What People Are Saying About Steve's R

Without Steve Murray's Reiki Program, I would still be declining in health, barely holding on to life, just barely. I can honestly say I would not be alive right now, had I not found Steve Murray's Reiki Books and Attunement DVDs. Steve, thank you does not seem like enough. ***N.L.***

While many books, DVDs, etc., say that they will reveal the secrets of Reiki, the series written by Steve Murray really delivers. Here you will learn all the Reiki symbols, the attunements for 1st level, second level, and Reiki master, and much, much, more. Thoughtfully written, you will find everything you want in this series of books. They are a must for any Reiki healer's library. ***P.T.***

This really helped me to find out what was holding me back from the financial and personal success I had been trying to achieve. Issues about feelings of unworthiness have been resolved now. I am so very grateful for all of Steve Murray's hard work and research on the behalf of others. Great Job! Another Fantastic Book from a true Master. ***K.H.***

I admit to being skeptical when I purchased Steve Murray's products: How could a Reiki Master justify passing the secret Reiki symbols on to the general public? But I feel that we live in different times now. To coin a phrase by Caroline Myss, there are now many "Mystics without monasteries." I am grateful that Steve has made attaining higher levels of Reiki practice available to those who cannot afford to go the traditional route. ***T.Y.***

This is a great way to learn Reiki. I have all of his books, DVDs, CDs. I can go back at anytime to study the information. This is well worth it, it teaches you the same thing a class does. It's amazing. I now have my Master through this wonderful program. ***D.F.***

Wow. It used to be, that receiving Reiki attunements was expensive, Reiki Masters were few and far between and Reiki knowledge was kept hush-hush (only known by a few). This book is amazing. Yes, I have been a Reiki Master for several years and when I wanted a thorough review, this book came to me. ***S.D.***

I took the Master Attunement via Murray's DVD, practiced his methods in the books, and can definitely feel a difference in the energy that channels through me. The energy in my hands went from pleasant warmth to almost an electrical current. Very powerful attunements! Namaste, ***M.B., R.N.***

I definitely recommend that anyone taking his attunements also read his Ultimate Guide Trilogy. They are so packed with information about Reiki that I feel so much more prepared to be a Reiki healer. They are truly wonderful and his "A Reiki 1st, Aura and Chakra" DVD is very helpful in showing you how to perform your own attunements. ***U.L.***

I have participated in face-to-face trainings and attunements, and have used Steve Murray's materials. Steve's work is as good, if not better, than the face-to-face presentations. I highly suggest you buy all of his materials if you are interested in Reiki. ***L.N.***

I would recommend Steve Murray's program for anyone that is interested in becoming a Reiki Healer or expanding their own knowledge and intensifying their own abilities as an energy healer. Steve Murray leaves no stone unturned, and will leave you feeling enlightened as an energy healer. ***M.C.***

Steve Murray's Reiki VOL 1,2,3 and Reiki False Beliefs and Attunement DVDs are nothing short of a miracle. They have helped me in my life and personal endeavors - more than I can say ***J.T.***

Reiki The Ultimate Guide Vol. 5

Learn New Psychic Attunements to Expand Psychic Gifts & Healing

Steve Murray

First Printing

Body & Mind Productions, Inc.

Reiki The Ultimate Guide Vol. 5
Learn New Psychic Attunements to
Expand Psychic Gifts & Healing

Published by
Body & Mind Productions
9429 Cedar Heights, Las Vegas, NV 89134
Website: www.healingreiki.com
Email: bodymindheal@aol.com

First Printing September 2008

Library of Congress Cataloging-in-Publication Data
Murray, Steve
Reiki the Ultimate Guide Vol. 5: Learn New Psychic Attunements to
Expand Psychic Gifts & Healing
/ Murray, Steve - 1st ed.
Library of Congress Control Number 2008904420
ISBN # 978-0-9792177-8-4
Includes bibliographical references and index.
1. Reiki 2. New Age 3. Alternative Health
4. Self-Healing 5. Spiritual 6. Healing

Cover design: Star Studios: Steve Lee
Photos: Star Studios: Edyta Sokolowska
Interior design: Star Studios, Edyta Sokolowska
Editors: Sonya Baity, Carol von Raesfeld

Printed in U.S.A.

DVDs-CDs-BOOKS

BOOKS BY STEVE MURRAY

Cancer Guided Imagery Program
For Radiation, Chemotherapy, Surgery, And Recovery

Reiki The Ultimate Guide
Learn Sacred Symbols and Attunements
Plus Reiki Secrets You Should Know

Reiki The Ultimate Guide Vol. 3
Learn New Reiki Aura
Attunements Heal Mental & Emotional Issues

Reiki The Ultimate Guide Vol. 4
Past Lives and Soul Retrieval
Remove Psychic Debris and Heal your life

Stop Eating Junk!
5 Minutes A Day-21 Day Program

Reiki The Ultimate Guide Vol. 2
Learn Reiki Healing with Chakras
plus New Reiki Attunements for All Levels

Reiki False Beliefs Exposed
For All Misinformation
Kept Secret By a Few Revealed

Reiki The Ultimate Guide Vol. 5
Learn New Psychic Attunements to Expand Psychic Abilities & Healing

DVDS BY STEVE MURRAY

Reiki Master Attunement
Become A Reiki Master

Reiki 2nd Level Attunement
Learn and Use the Reiki Sacred Symbols

A Reiki 1st
Aura and Chakra
Attunement Performed

Successfully Preparing for Cancer Radiation
Guided Imagery and Subliminal Program

Preparing Mentally & Emotionally For Cancer Surgery
A Guided Imagery Program

Preparing Mentally & Emotionally For Cancer Radiation
A Guided Imagery Program

Reiki 1st Level Attunement
Give Healing Energy To Yourself and Others

Reiki PsychicAttunement
Open and Expand Your Psychic Abilities

Reiki Healing Attunement
Heal Emotional-Mental-Physical-Spiritual Issues

Reiki Psychic Attunement Vol. 2
New Attunements to Expand Psychic Abilities

Preparing Mentally & Emotionally For Cancer Chemotherapy
A Guided Imagery Program

Preparing Mentally & Emotionally For Cancer Recovery
A Guided Imagery Program

Pain Relief Subliminal Program
Let Your Unconscious Mind Do It

Destroying Cancer Cells
Guided Imagery and Subliminal Program

30-Day Subliminal Weight Loss Program Let Your Unconscious Mind Do The Work!

Cancer Fear and Stress Relief Program

Successfully Preparing for Cancer Chemotherapy
Guided Imagery and Subliminal Program

MUSIC CDs BY STEVE MURRAY

Reiki Healing Music Attunement Volume I

Reiki Healing Music Attunement Volume II

Reiki Psychic Music Attunement Volume I

Reiki Psychic Music Attunement Volume II

Reiki Aura Music Attunement

Reiki Chakra Music Attunement

DVDs BY BODY & MIND PRODUCTIONS

Learning To Read The Tarot Intuitively

Learning To Read The Symbolism Of The Tarot

Mind Fitness Workout:
"Program the Mind for Weight Loss as you Exercise" Dance Workout

How to Contact Spirits, Angels &
Departed Loved Ones:
A step-by-step Guide

Mind Fitness Workout:
"Program the Mind for Weight Loss as you Exercise" Walking Workout

How to Contact Spirits Vol. 2
Learn to use a Spirit/Ouija Board and Hold a Séance

Mind Fitness Workout:
"Program the Mind for Weight Loss as you Exercise" Fitness Workout

This book is dedicated to

All open-minded Reiki Healers around the world

Steve's Reiki Mission Statement

To make Reiki knowledge, guidance and Attunements available to everyone that seeks them. To make Reiki 1st, 2nd and Master Level Attunements affordable for everyone, so healing can be spread throughout the world.

Steve Murray

CONTENTS

The intuitive mind is a sacred gift and the rational mind is a faithful servant. We have created a society that honors the servant and has forgotten the gift.

- Albert Einstein

Introduction

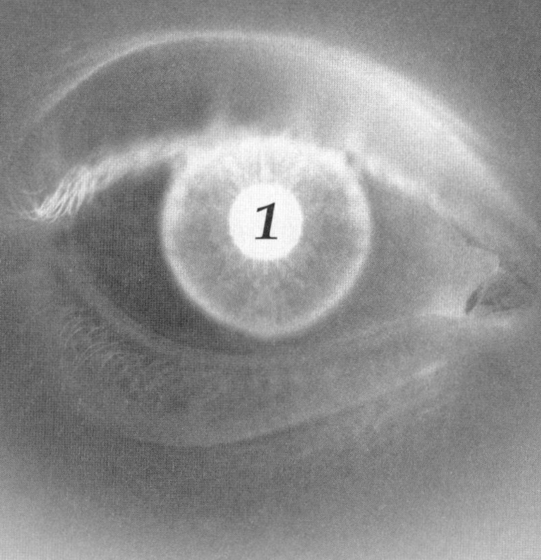

Opening

If you are reading this book, there's a good chance you have already learned how to pass a Reiki Psychic Attunement[1] from the book "Reiki the Ultimate Guide: Learn Sacred Symbols & Attunements plus Reiki Secrets You Should

[1] Attunement - a sacred process, initiation and/or meditation with a specific purpose and intent performed by a Spiritual Master.

Know." Better yet, you have received a Reiki Psychic Attunement from the DVD "Reiki Psychic Attunement: Open and Expand Your Psychic Abilities."

If you are not familiar with this attunement, let me explain that the Reiki Psychic Attunement helps clear your mental, spiritual, physical and emotional bodies so psychic abilities (gifts) can surface and/or expand. This attunement has successfully opened and expanded psychic abilities for tens of thousands of people around the world.

If you have received the Reiki Psychic Attunement and are ready to take your psychic abilities to the next level, this book offers that opportunity. If you have not received the Psychic Attunement, I strongly recommend taking it before or soon after receiving any attunements in this guide. This will ensure the best results for expanding your psychic abilities and giving the attunements to others.

What You Will Learn

There are three distinct psychic abilities: Clairvoyance, Clairaudience, and Clairsentience. In this Ultimate Guide you will learn how to perform a specific Reiki Psychic Attunement[2] on yourself or others to expand each one of these abilities, which will help with healing yourself and others. In addition, you will also discover positive and negative Psychic Cords that can be attached to your Chakras, and how they can impact your health.

[2] The DVD "Reiki Psychic Attunement Vol. 2 New Attunements to Expand Psychic Abilities" will actually pass the three specific Psychic Attunements to you. But the DVD does not show the steps on how to perform the attunements included in this book.

Most significantly, you will learn to detect if you have a negative Psychic Cord, and if so, how to disconnect it to eliminate any healing issues the connection might be creating. And finally, there is a segment on how to contact your Spirit Guide(s) with a Reiki Spirit Board.

As with all of my books, I like to keep them simple and focused on the teachings, and this one is not an exception. Before we begin the teachings I will give an overview of psychic abilities.

Psychic Abilities

Psychic abilities are different ways of receiving information from other than our five normal senses: sight, smell, taste, hearing and touch. Everybody has psychic abilities to a certain degree, but not everybody is aware of their abilities. When a person expands their psychic abilities he or she will have access to additional mental, physical, spiritual and emotional information that will help with Reiki healing for themselves and others. Also, with expanded psychic abilities, a person is more intuitive and able to make correct decisions and choices in the daily routine of life.

Psychic information from these abilities comes from many sources. Some of these sources may include Spirit Guides, Angels, the Astral Plane, Akashic Records, past lives, future events and the Universal Mind or Consciousness. And I'm sure there are sources from which psychic information originates that we are not yet aware of or are able to comprehend. Okay, let's get started on expanding your psychic abilities.

Everyone is born with psychic abilities. It's just a matter of knowing how to tap into it.

- Mettrie

Attunement

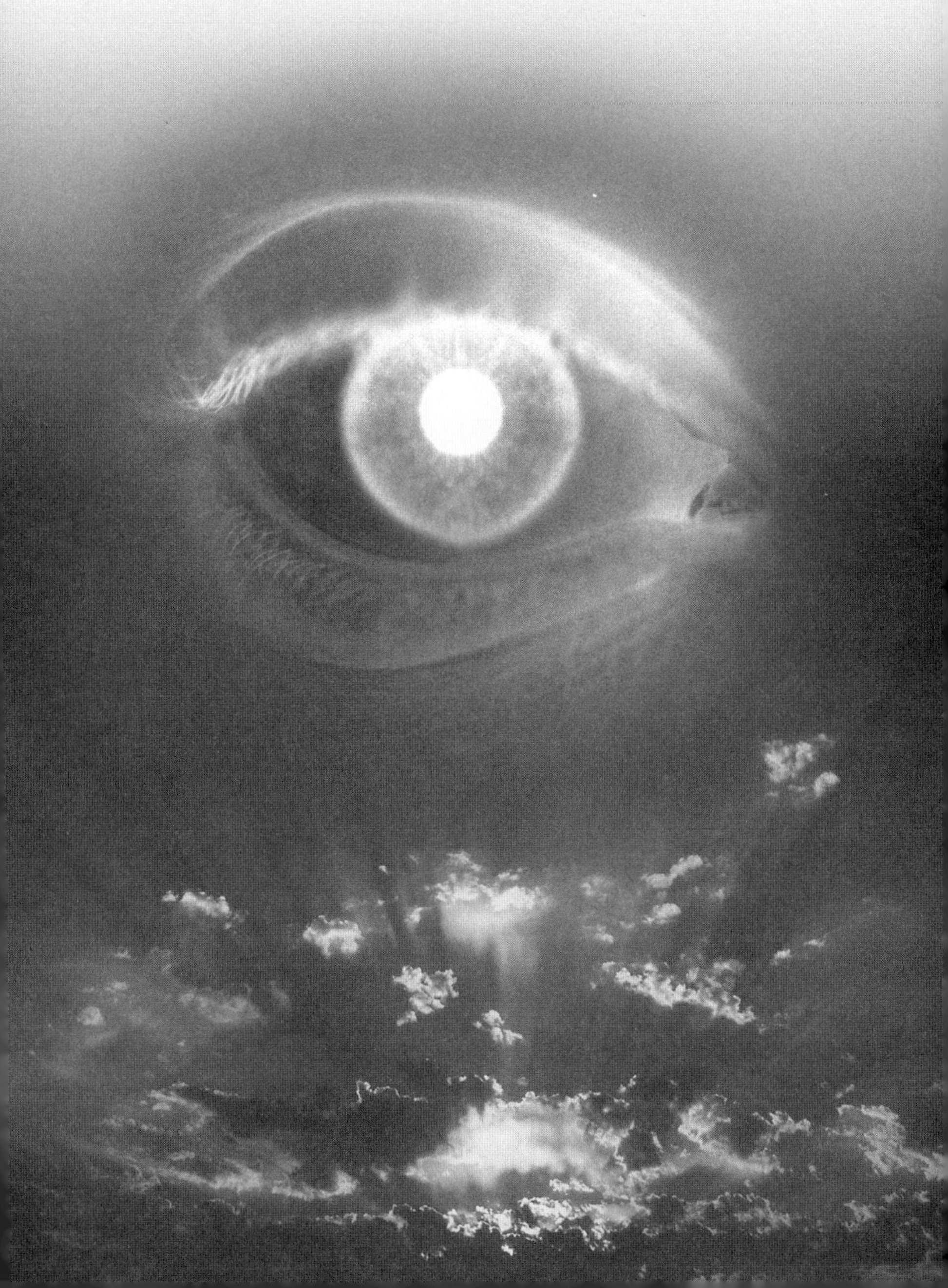

Everyone who is born to the Earth has a psychic ability lying dormant.

- Derek Acorah

Attunement Overview

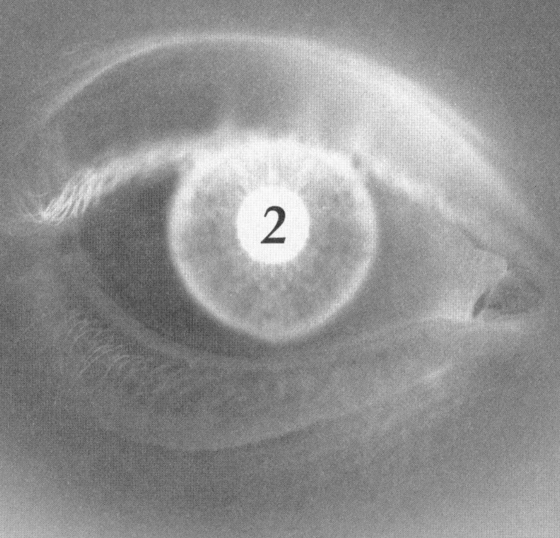

Two Questions

There are two questions that are always on a person's mind before they receive a Psychic Attunement: What can I expect during a Psychic Attunement? and, most frequently asked, What can I expect after the attunement? This chapter has the answers.

During the Attunement

When receiving a Psychic Attunement, you may feel heat or experience tingling sensations; see colors, visions or symbols; hear voices; experience specific or general aromas; feel energized; and/or you might have visions. Your whole body may feel lighter and the attunement may seem like a dream. Some people are preoccupied during the attunement and consciously do not experience anything. Each person will have his or her own individual experience during a Psychic Attunement, and it can be different each time an attunement is received. But no matter what your experience, you will have received the Psychic Attunement successfully when it is performed.

After the Attunement

After receiving a Psychic Attunement your psychic ability will increase from whatever level the psychic ability was at before you received the attunement. For example, if a person is mildly clairvoyant, they will now receive stronger, clearer pictures or images after the attunement. Or, if a person receives information in dreams, he or she will experience more informative and clearer dreams. In other words, every person will have their own unique increase in a psychic ability after the Psychic Attunement.

Also you might not be consciously aware of any increase or shift of a psychic ability after receiving an attunement, but that does not mean it is not happening. The majority of the time there will be a gradual increasing of the psychic ability for which you received the attunement. And there is always a chance you can experience dramatically improved psychic abilities right away after taking the attunement. As previously mentioned, everyone will have a different result after the attunement.

Attunement Caveats

Reiki Psychic Attunements do not give you instant psychic ability, although it appears that way with a few people immediately after taking the attunement. This is because the attunement opened and/or expanded a psychic ability they were unaware they had. However, there is caution with receiving Psychic Attunements. On occasion, a person will take a Psychic Attunement over and over in a brief period of time for various reasons, including wanting to become psychic as fast as they can. He or she will then start receiving too much psychic information at once and be unable to process it, thus becoming unbalanced. Once the attunements are stopped, the information will slow down and the person will become balanced again. So, with this understanding, only take one specific attunement once every two-weeks and see what unfolds. Although I do not recommend it, you can take all three specific Psychic Attunements within a two-week period. Just don't repeat the same attunement in that time period. Be patient when developing your psychic abilities and take an attunement as many times as you feel is necessary using the two-week guideline.

All three psychic abilities are equally important even though you might be naturally stronger in one of the three already. If this is true of your psychic situation, don't fixate on developing that one ability over the other two because it is easier for you. Take the Psychic Attunement for the ability you perceive is the strongest first and practice using it. Then take the other two attunements so your psychic abilities will be balanced. You need to be receptive to all three psychic abilities, because in healing situations, you never know how the psychic information will be made available.

And I think we'll be able to prove scientifically that other talents such as intuitive, psychic, Clairvoyant are very real.

- Shirley Maclaine

There is a discipline, a spiritual code that you should adhere to, that you do not hurt anyone in any way shape or form either mentally or physically.

- Derek Acorah

Attunement Guidelines

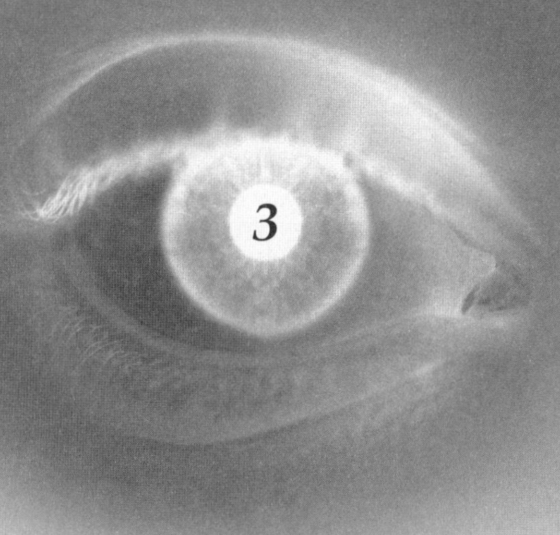

Reiki Symbols

Reiki Symbols[3] will be used during the Reiki Psychic Attunements. I assume you know the symbols or are at least aware of them. The Reiki Symbols that I use during the Reiki Psychic Attunements are the classic Usui Symbols from the Usui lineage.

[3] Starting on page 207, the four Reiki Symbols are shown and explained.

In reading the directions for performing a Reiki Psychic Attunement, you might discover the Reiki Symbols you use look different than those illustrated here. This difference[4] can include symbols with different lines, extra lines, and lines that go in reverse directions. If this is the case, do not worry. The Reiki Symbols you received from your Reiki Master are the right symbols for you to use because you have been attuned to them. What is important is your intent when using the Reiki Symbols to which you have been attuned. With that in mind, if your Reiki Symbols do have variations, just use them in place of the ones I use during the attunements.

Visualize and Activate

In the Psychic Attunement directions, I ask you to visualize and activate Reiki Symbols. Visualization in this case is seeing Reiki Symbols in your mind's eye in various locations, in front of specific Chakras (Photo 1). Some Healers have a challenge visualizing, and I am one of them. If you have a difficult time visualizing, just imagine or know the symbols are in front of the Chakra, or you can draw them in the air like I do (Photo 2).

When you activate a Reiki Symbol, it means to turn it on, make it work, put it into action, etc. There are many ways to activate a Reiki Symbol, and it depends on the way you were taught or your preference. A few ways to activate a symbol are thinking of its name, saying it aloud, or silently if non-attuned people are present, or you can just

[4] There are more in-depth explanations for the reasons behind the Reiki Symbols and their variations in "Reiki Ultimate Guide Vol.1 and Reiki False Beliefs Exposed For All."

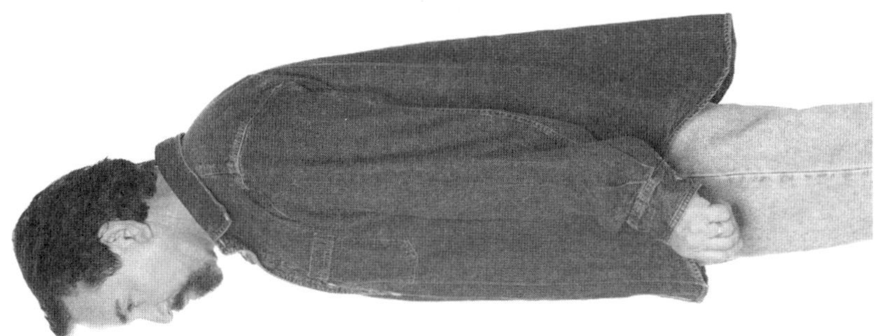

Photo 1

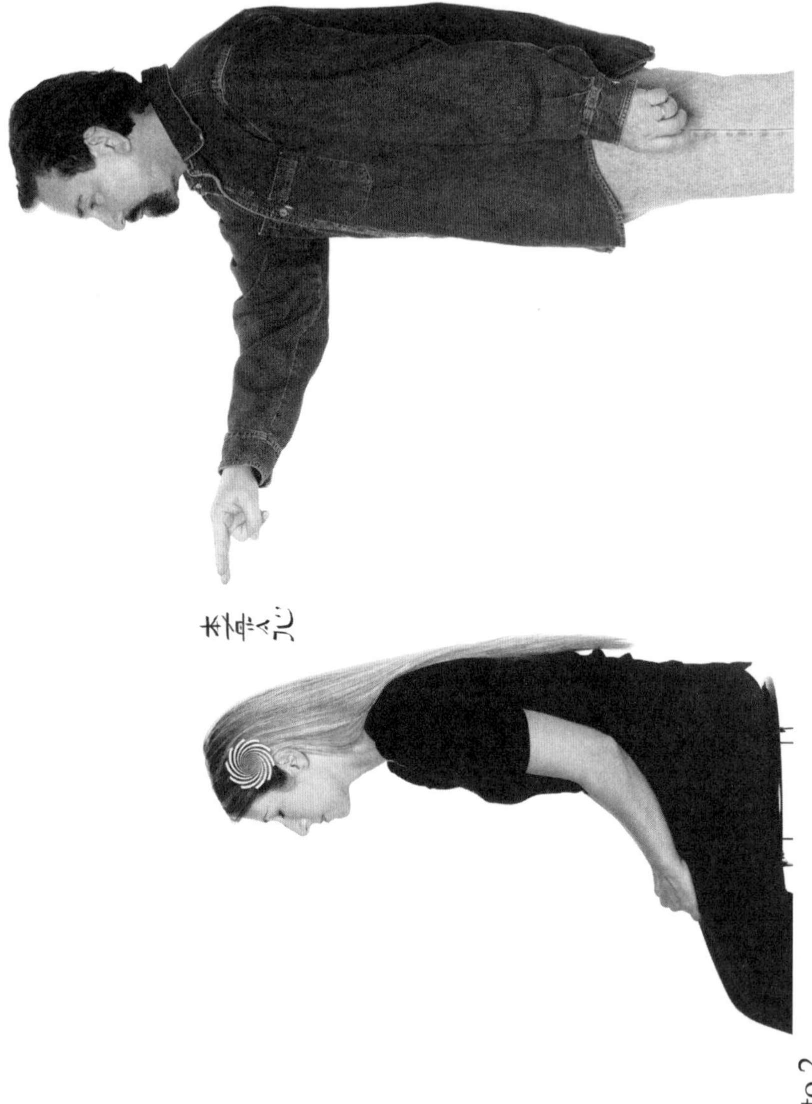

Photo 2

use your intent to activate the symbol. There is no "correct" or "incorrect" way to use or activate these symbols as long as the intent is there, so activate Reiki Symbols the way that works best for you. At various points in the Psychic Attunement Steps you will need to visualize a Reiki Symbol and then activate it. This is done almost simultaneously. In fact, when some Healers visualize a symbol, it's activated automatically.

Embed the Symbol

Once you have the Reiki Symbol visualized and activated in front of the Chakra called for in the directions, the next step is to embed the symbol into that Chakra. This means to move (place) the symbol into the Chakra in the physical body. You do this by visualizing the symbol moving into this Chakra (Photo 3). Again, if you have a hard time visualizing, as an option you can guide the symbol with your hand (Photo 4) into the Chakra. Or just know the symbol has been successfully placed (Photo 5) in the Chakra with your intent.

Intent

Intent is an anticipated outcome that guides your planned actions mentally, spiritually, or physically to make the outcome manifest, that is, become a physical reality. Reiki is an intent-focused healing system. Strong and focused intent is the key to successfully using Reiki in healing sessions and passing attunements. For example, if you are performing a Reiki Psychic Clairvoyance Attunement, your main intent is to expand the Clairvoyance of the person who is receiving the attunement; this includes

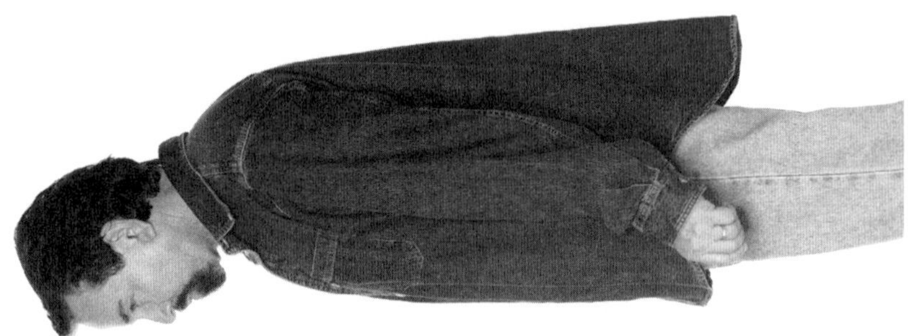

Photo 3

Photo 4

Photo 5

yourself if you are performing a self-attunement. When passing any one of the Psychic Attunements, the intent of the attunement, the purpose for which it is being given, is the key to a successful Psychic Attunement.

Self-Attunement

Self-Attunement directions are given for all three Psychic Attunements. With these attunements you will need to be able to visualize the Reiki Symbols when working with your Back Chakras. Self-Attunements will work, but sometimes it is easier to have a friend or relative give you the Psychic Attunement from the directions in the book or receive the Psychic Attunements from my DVD.

Chakras

Make sure during the Psychic Attunement you work with the Chakras in the correct sequence. You will notice the Chakra that is associated with the Psychic ability for which the attunement is given receives the most Reiki Symbols and focus during the attunement. For example, Clairvoyance is associated with the Sixth Chakra, so the Sixth Chakra receives the most symbols and is the main focus during the Psychic Clairvoyance Attunement. The back Chakras of each major Chakra corresponds to our unconscious non-physical being and to the laws of the non-physical universe. That is why they are predominately used in the Psychic Attunements. The front side of each major Chakra corresponds to our conscious being and the laws of the physical universe.

Meditation

To help expand your psychic abilities after receiving a Psychic Attunement you need to learn to alter your state of consciousness, which is done by lowering and slowing down your brain frequency. Meditation is the best way to do this. If you meditate now, keep doing so. If not, I highly suggest you learn to meditate.

Meditation can be done with or without music, using various breathing techniques, in any area, at any time of the day or night. Meditations with mantras and chants will also work. Discover the meditation technique that works best for you and meditate as often as you can. You will indeed find your psychic abilities expanding faster with the practice of meditation.

We need to let our intuition guide us,
and then be willing to follow
that guidance directly and fearlessly.

- Shakti Gawain

There is a soul force in the universe, which, if we permit it, will flow through us and produce miraculous results.

- Mahatma Gandhi

Attunement Preparations

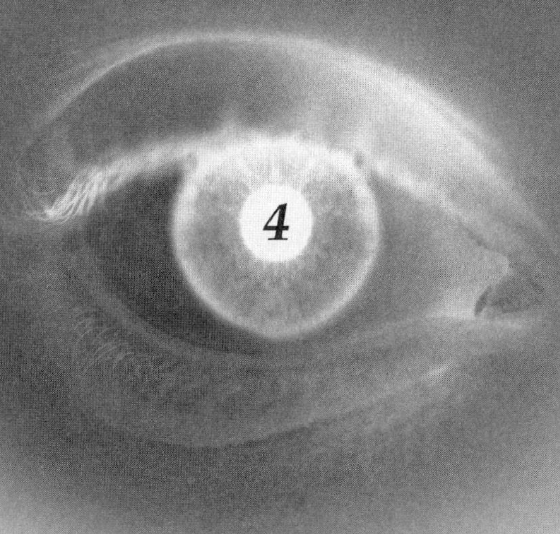

The Steps

There are steps in preparing for, and steps to take after the Reiki Psychic Attunements. And the same steps are followed for self-attunements. They are similar to the steps[5] used when performing a Reiki Level (1st, 2nd, Master), Aura, Chakra and Healing Attunement, with a few variations.

[5] The steps in the Reiki The Ultimate Guides Vol. 1-4. Even if you are already knowledgeable about performing these steps, please review them anyway before proceeding to the next chapter.

Preparing for the Attunement

Follow these suggestions before receiving or giving a Psychic Attunement. The attunement will still be passed and received even if you cannot follow every suggestion, but do as many as you can to ensure that the attunement is as effective as possible.

- Establish at least 24 hours before performing a Psychic Attunement who (this includes yourself) is going to receive a Psychic Attunement, which attunement, and where and when the attunement will be performed. This will help build and create a stronger intent when the Psychic Attunement is performed.

- Since you have established ahead of time when and where the attunement will be held, send Reiki (using the Long Distance symbol - Hon Sha Ze Sho Nen) to the room where the Psychic Attunement will take place. Send this Reiki with the intent to start clearing the area of any Psychic Debris[6] that might be there.

- Limit or stop eating all animal protein 24 hours before the attunement.

- Stop drinking alcohol 24 hours before the attunement.

- Limit sugar 24 hours before the attunement.

- Limit or stop smoking at least four to six hours before the attunement.

---

[6] On pages 211 and 212, Psychic Debris is fully explained.

- Consume only water or juice four to six hours before the attunement.

- Limit or stop using caffeinated drinks four to six hours before the attunement.

Before Passing the Attunement

1. Wash hands. This is a simple step and often neglected, but an important step even if you are going to perform the attunement on yourself. Just like a medical professional, a Reiki Healer is always working with their hands, so they must be clean. The easiest way is to buy disposable cleaning packets or a dispenser with antibacterial gel.

2. You have already sent Reiki to the area where the attunement will be performed with the intent to start clearing any Psychic Debris that might be there. Now you must make sure that all Psychic Debris has been completely dissolved before the attunement. If, by chance, there still happens to be some lingering Psychic Debris present, it could become attached to the Aura or Chakras of the persons giving or receiving the Psychic Attunement. If this did occur, the kind of health problems that might develop depends on the source of the Psychic Debris left in the room. Some of the symptoms of Psychic Debris attachment are feeling drained, sick, and/or feeling strange emotions to which you are unaccustomed to. So for protection, do one or both of the following steps with the intent to clear the room of any Psychic Debris:

- Visualize or imagine white or golden light filling the area where the session will be performed.

- Smudge or sage the room.

3. The person performing and the person receiving the Psychic Attunement should ground themselves before the attunement. This will make sure all the Chakras are clear and balanced during the attunement. Experienced Healers usually have their own favorite method for grounding. If you have one, feel free to use it in this step. Or you can use this simple and effective method I always use for grounding.

- Stand straight, and bring Reiki through the top of your head (7th Chakra) all the way down through your body, then out both legs into the earth (Illus. 1). Wait a few seconds, then bring it back from the earth, all the way back up both legs and out the top of your head (Illus. 2). This whole process only takes a few minutes.

4. Right before you start a Reiki Psychic Attunement you must do two things:

- Make your intent clear on which attunement you are going to perform. For example, if you are going to give a Reiki Psychic Clairvoyance Attunement, you state "I am about to give a Psychic Clairvoyance Attunement to John Smith." You do this silently and it should only take a few seconds. You can use your own wording as long as the intent is clear.

- Ask your Higher Power, Source, Guardian Angel, Universal Mind, Spirit Guide, etc., for guidance during the attunement.

Illus. 1

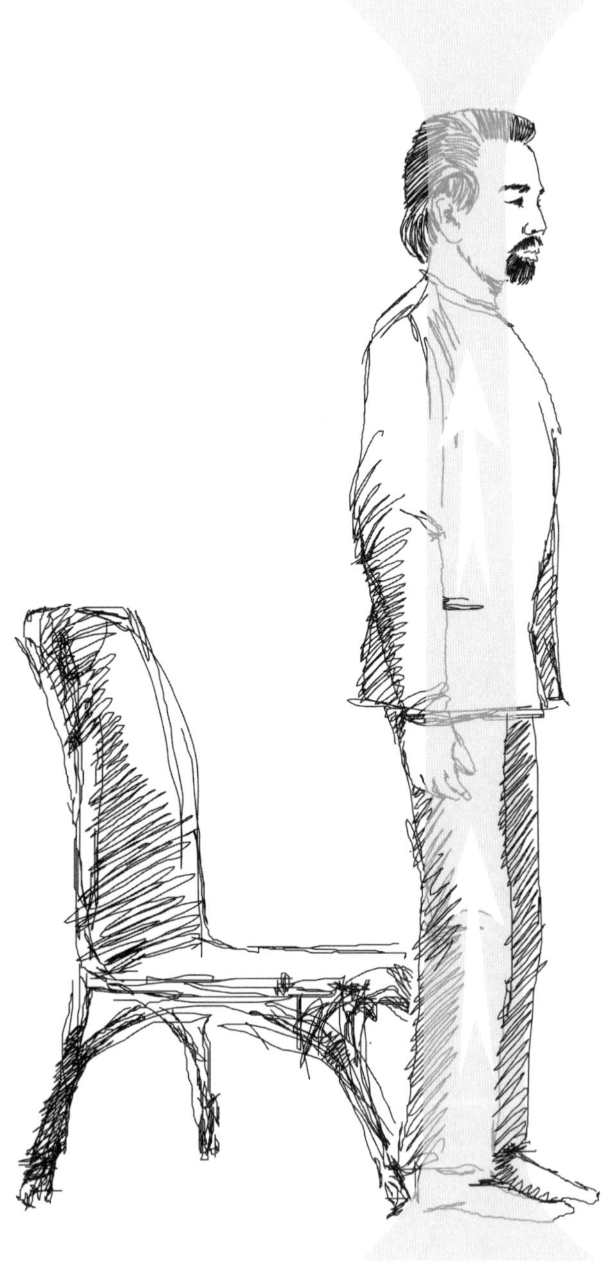

Illus. 2

After the Psychic Attunement

1. After performing a Psychic Attunement, rub and shake your hands to break any energetic connection you might have formed with the Aura and/or Chakra(s) of the person receiving the attunement.

2. Psychic Debris can be released during any Reiki Attunement. In fact, you want that to happen to facilitate with healing. The amount of debris released (if any) during an attunement can vary depending on the individual and his or her condition and circumstances. You cleared the room of Psychic Debris prior to the attunement, now you need to clear the area again where the attunement was performed, as well as from yourself and the person who received the attunement. To accomplish this, do the following:

- While the person who received the attunement is still in the room, visualize (or know) white or golden light coming into the room, filling it up and surrounding both of you. And at the same time the light is filling the room, ask your source (God, Higher Power, Higher Consciousness, etc.) that any and all Psychic Debris present be removed and dissolved from the room, yourself and the person who received the attunement.

3. Wash your hands. As I mentioned before, the easiest way is to use disposable cleaning packets or a dispenser with antibacterial gel.

4. Sleep and Rest. After receiving a Psychic Attunement take a warm shower and sleep. This allows the Aura and Chakras to integrate the Psychic Attunement without other distractions.

Our eyes believe themselves, our ears believe other people, and our intuition believes the truth of the spirit.

- German Proverb

Clairaudience

I think people will become more and more aware that we are all more than we seem.

- Shirley Maclaine

Clairaudience Review

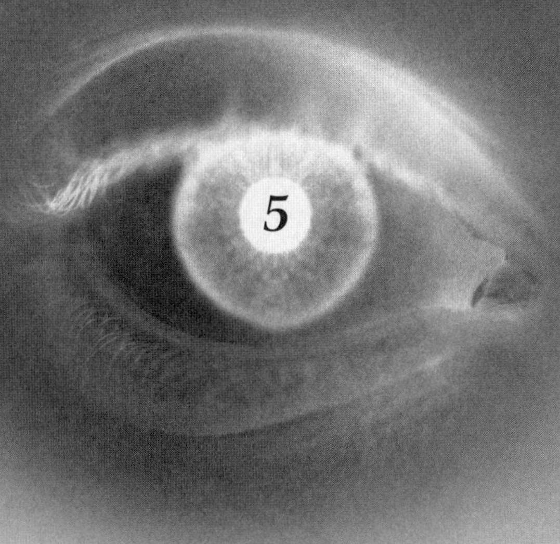

Clairaudience Defined

Clairaudience is referred to as "clear hearing" or having "psychic ears" and is associated with the 5th Chakra. It is the psychic ability of hearing information. This psychic information can be heard from within your body, within your mind, or outside your body and mind.

Each person will experience this ability differently. The experience can be hearing thoughts, a clear distinct voice, or hearing only letters and syllables. A person with expanded Clairaudience can sometimes hear sounds like horns, kids playing or a dog barking. Sometimes a person might not actually hear sounds, but have only a mental perception of sound in what is called a "mental ear."

Clairaudience Manifesting

There are two common ways Clairaudience can manifest. The first is hearing a clear voice that speaks directly to you. For example, you hear a voice telling you to make a stop at the next corner instead of just walking non-stop across the street. Even though you do not see any cars, you heed the voice, and a car seems to appear out of nowhere and speeds across the street, thus saving you from injury.

The second way Clairaudience can manifest is the most frequent; it is the ability to "hear" thoughts. For example, you are trying to solve a personal dilemma and you hear a thought giving you advice. A person will sometimes refer to hearing thoughts as "a little voice inside my head," unaware that they have tapped into their Clairaudience, an ability they didn't know they had.

In reality, people are receiving thoughts they can hear throughout the day, but their Clairaudience is not developed, so they are not aware of these messages. By expanding your Clairaudient ability, you will be able to hear the source or root cause, and location of the healing challenge with yourself or another person. And, you will be able to hear healing options and directions to help with healing challenges.

The only real valuable thing is intuition.
- Albert Einstein

Intuition comes very close to clairvoyance; it appears to be the extrasensory perception of reality

- Alexis Carrel

Clairaudience Attunement

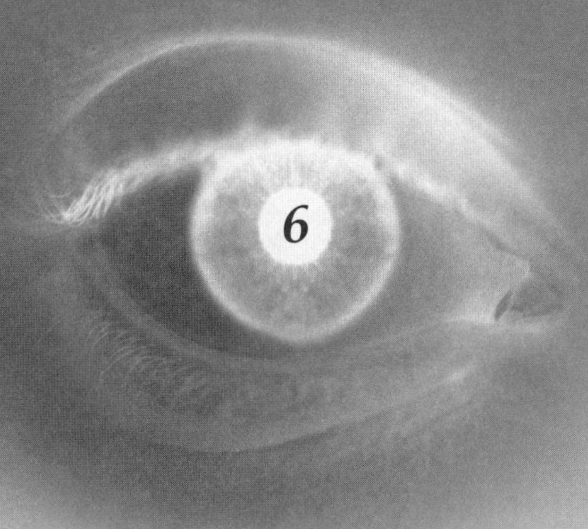

Giving the Clairaudience Attunement Step-by-Step

1. State prayer and intent for the attunement.

2. Place both of your hands over the Sixth Chakra (Photo 6) for about a minute with the intent to clear it.

Photo 6

From the Back

3. Draw or visualize Sei He Ki, the Emotional Symbol, over the Seventh Chakra (Photo 7), activate it and then embed[7] the symbol into the Chakra.

4. Draw or visualize Dai Koo Myo, the Master Symbol, in front of the Fifth Chakra (Photo 8), activate it and embed the symbol into the Chakra.

5. Draw or visualize Hon Sha Ze Sho Nen, the Long Distance Symbol, in front of the Fifth Chakra (Photo 9), activate it and embed the symbol into the Chakra.

6. Draw or visualize the Emotional Symbol in front of the Fifth Chakra (Photo 10), activate it and embed the symbol into the Chakra.

7. Draw or visualize Cho Ku Rei, the Power Symbol, in front of the First Chakra (Photo 11), activate it and embed the symbol into the Chakra.

8. Draw or visualize the Power Symbol in front of the Sixth Chakra (Photo 12), activate it and embed the symbol into the Chakra.

9. Channel Reiki into the Fifth Chakra for a few minutes (Photo 13).

---

[7] How to activate and embed Reiki Symbols are explained on pages 24 and 27.

Photo 7

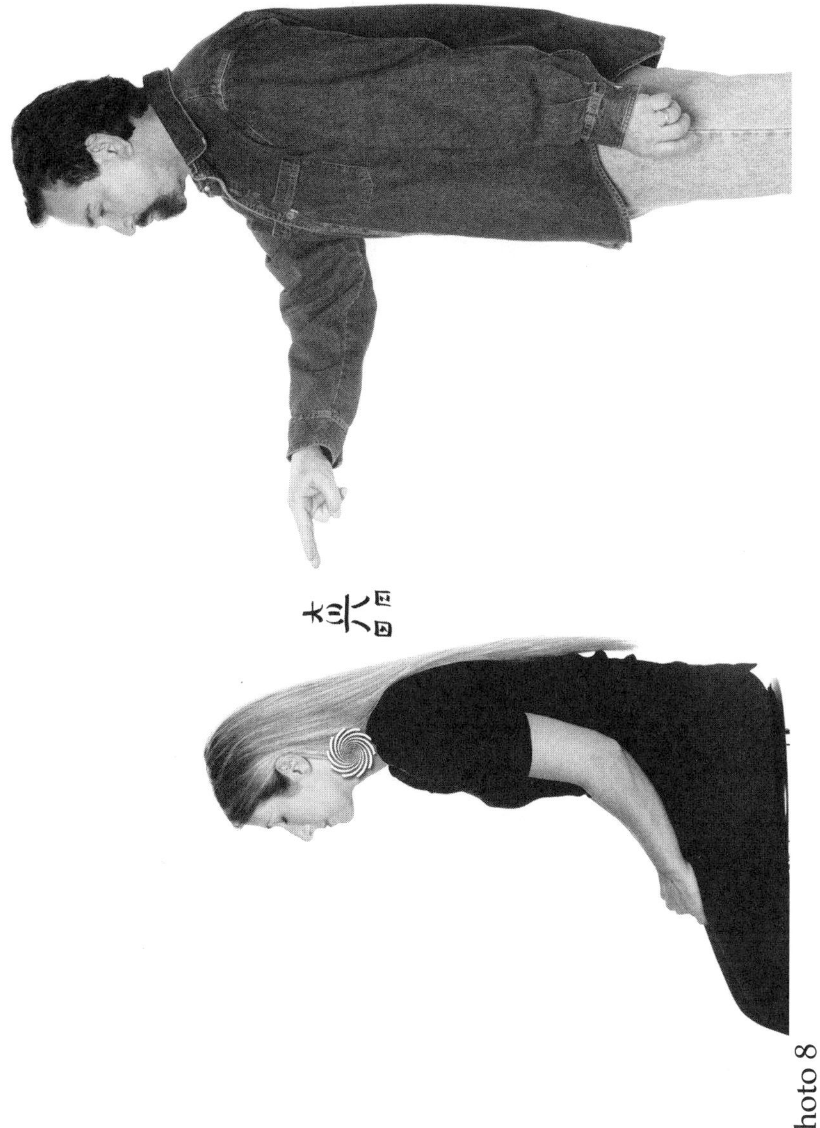

Photo 8

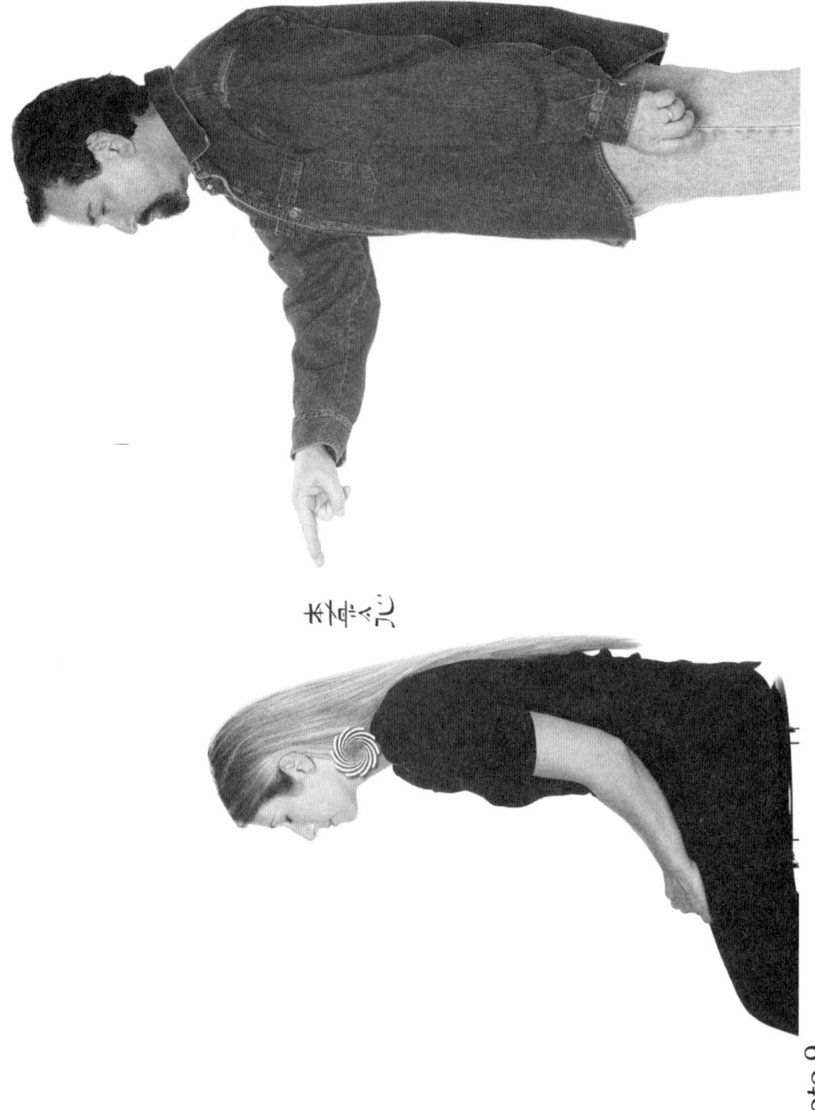

Photo 9

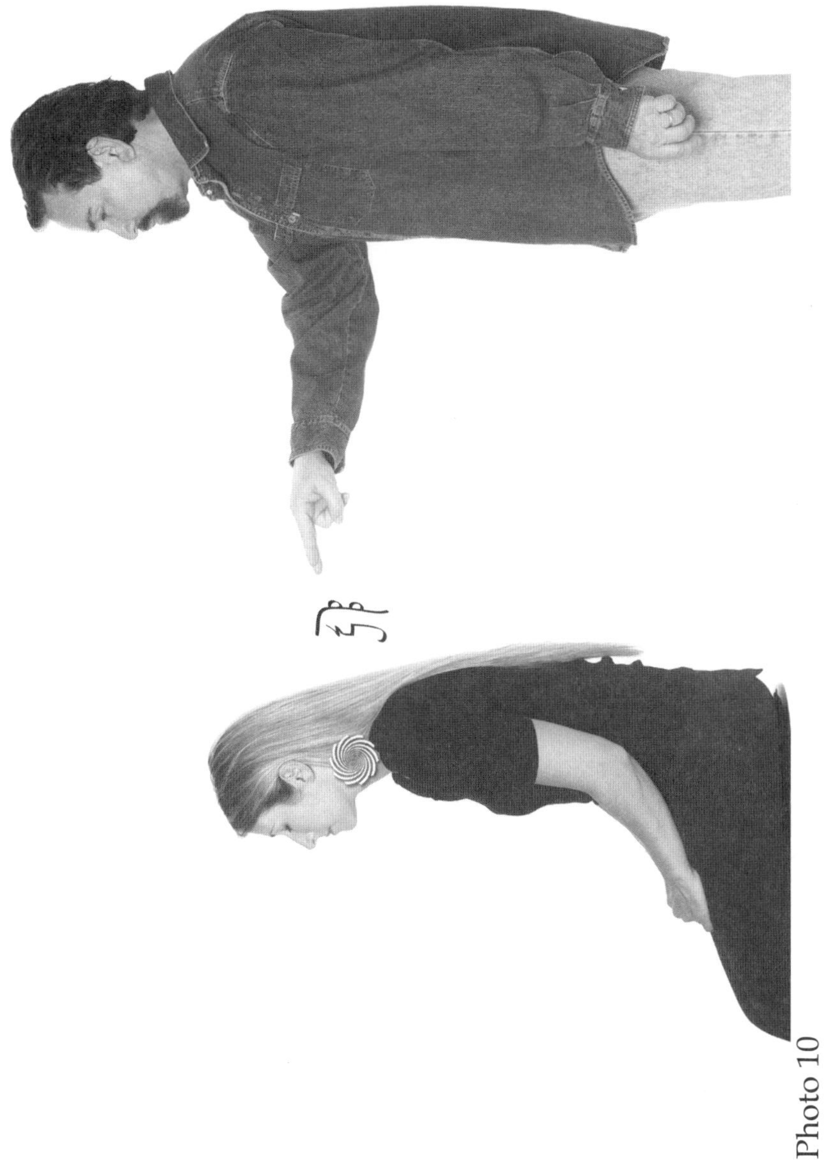

Photo 10

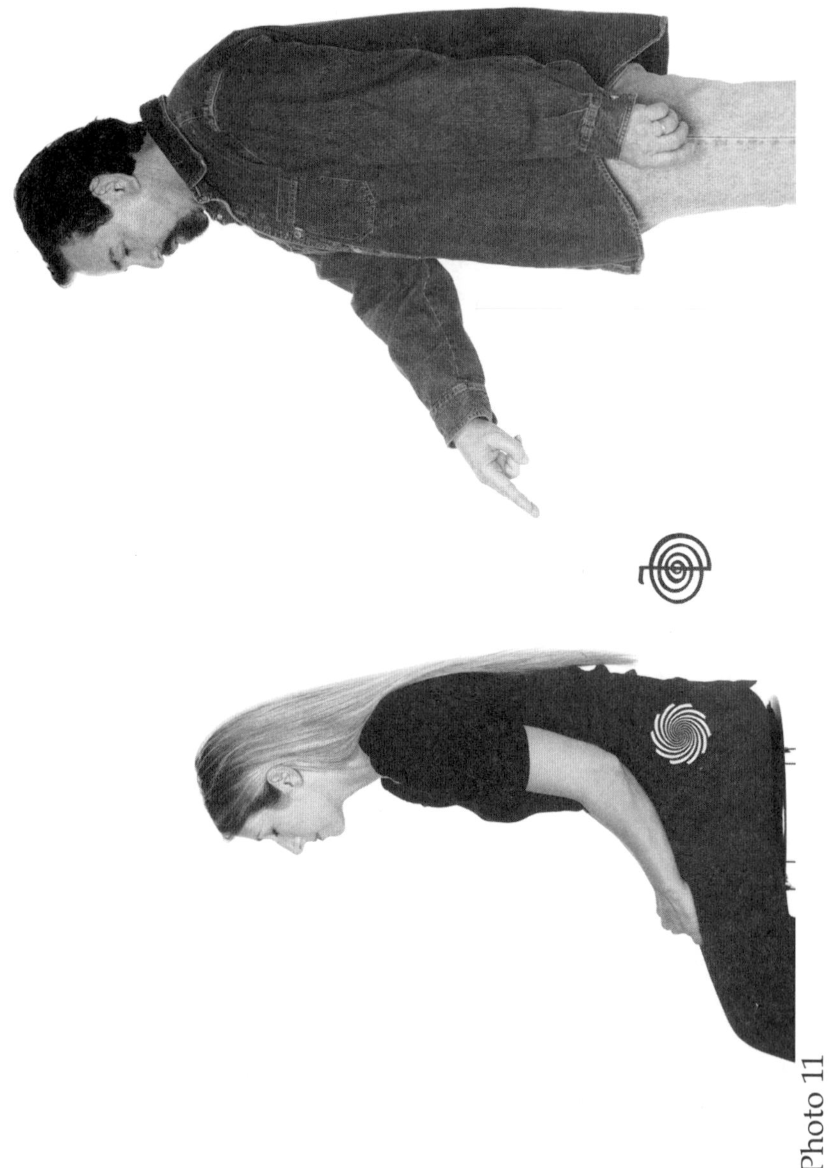

Photo 11

Photo 12

Photo 13

From the Front

10. Draw or visualize the Power Symbol in front of the Fifth Chakra (Photo 14), activate it and embed the symbol into the Chakra.

11. Draw or visualize the Power Symbol in front of the First Chakra (Photo 15), activate it and embed the symbol into the Chakra.

12. Draw or visualize the Power Symbol in front of the Sixth Chakra (Photo 16), activate it and embed the symbol into the Chakra.

13. Channel Reiki into the Fifth Chakra for a few minutes (Photo 17).

14. Have the person receiving the attunement open their eyes (Photo 18), the attunement is complete.

Photo 14

Photo 15

Photo 16

Photo 17

Photo 18

Clairaudience Self-Attunement Step-by-Step

1. State prayer and the intent for the attunement

2. Place a hand over the Sixth Chakra for about a minute with the intent to clear it (Photo 19).

From the Back

3. Visualize Sei He Ki, the Emotional Symbol, over the Seventh Chakra (Photo 20), activate it and embed the symbol into the Chakra.

4. Visualize Dai Koo Myo, the Master Symbol, in front of the Fifth Chakra (Photo 21), activate it and embed the symbol into the Chakra.

5. Visualize Hon Sha Ze Sho Nen, the Long Distance Symbol, in front of the Fifth Chakra (Photo 22), activate it and embed the symbol into the Chakra.

6. Visualize the Emotional Symbol in front of the Fifth Chakra (Photo 23), activate it and embed the symbol into the Chakra.

7. Visualize Cho Ku Rei, the Power Symbol, in front of the First Chakra (Photo 24), activate it and embed the symbol into the Chakra.

8. Visualize the Power Symbol in front of the Sixth Chakra (Photo 25), activate it and embed the symbol into the Chakra.

Photo 19

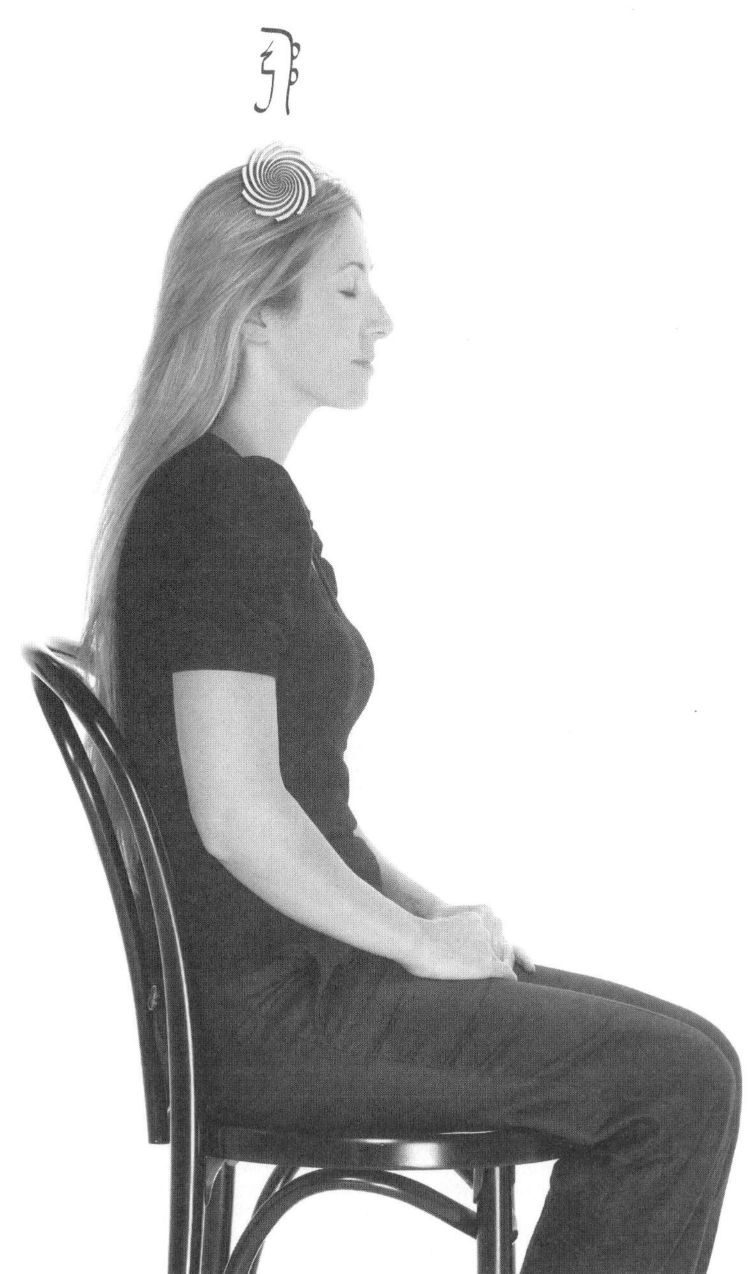

Photo 20

Photo 21

Photo 22

Photo 23

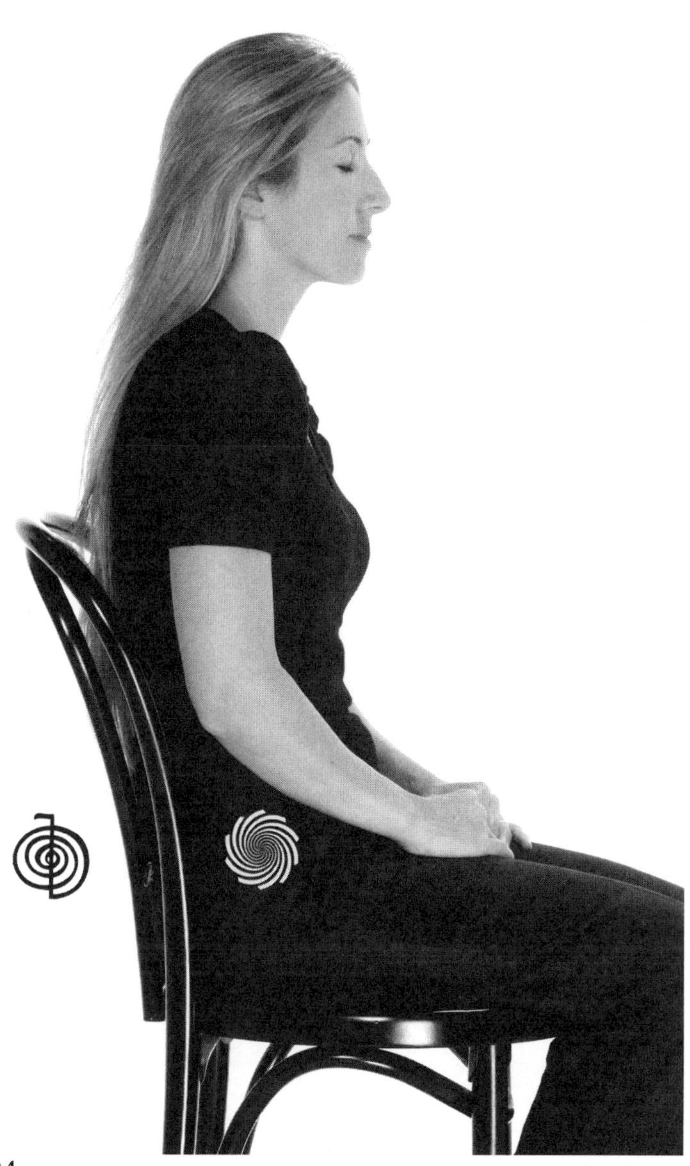

Photo 24

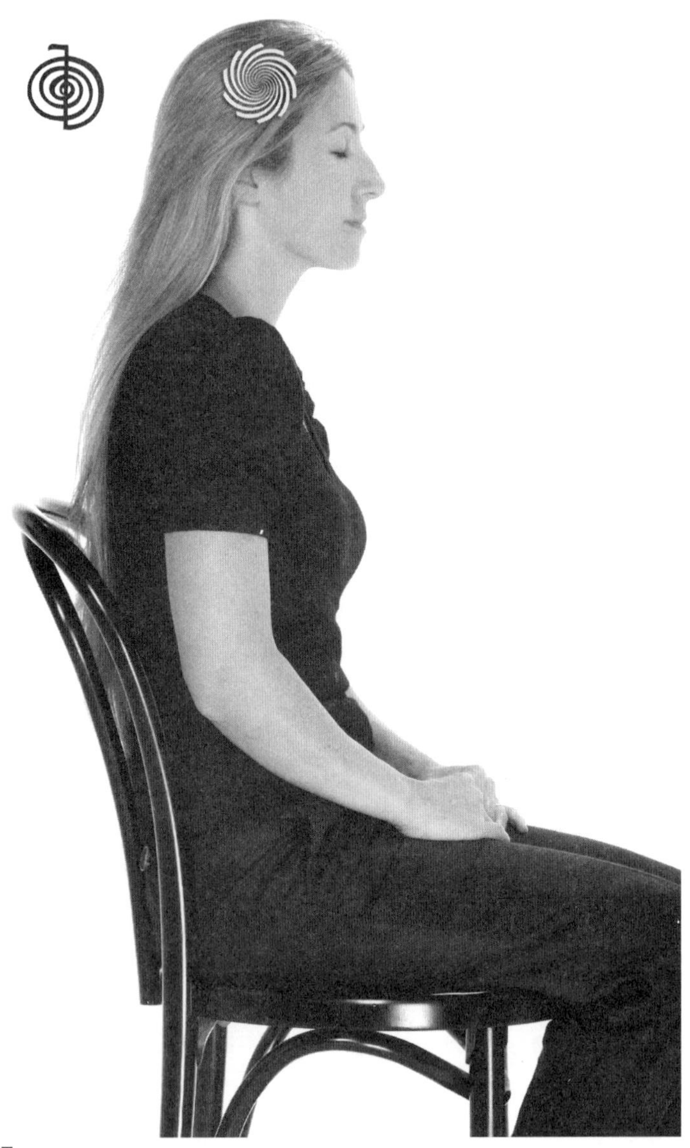

Photo 25

From the Front

9. Visualize the Power Symbol in front of the Fifth Chakra (Photo 26), activate it and embed the symbol into the Chakra.

10. Visualize the Power Symbol in front of the First Chakra (Photo 27), activate it and embed the symbol into the Chakra.

11. Visualize the Power Symbol in front of the Sixth Chakra (Photo 28), activate it and embed the symbol into the Chakra.

12. Channel Reiki into the Fifth Chakra for a few minutes (Photo 29).

13. Open your eyes, the attunement is complete.

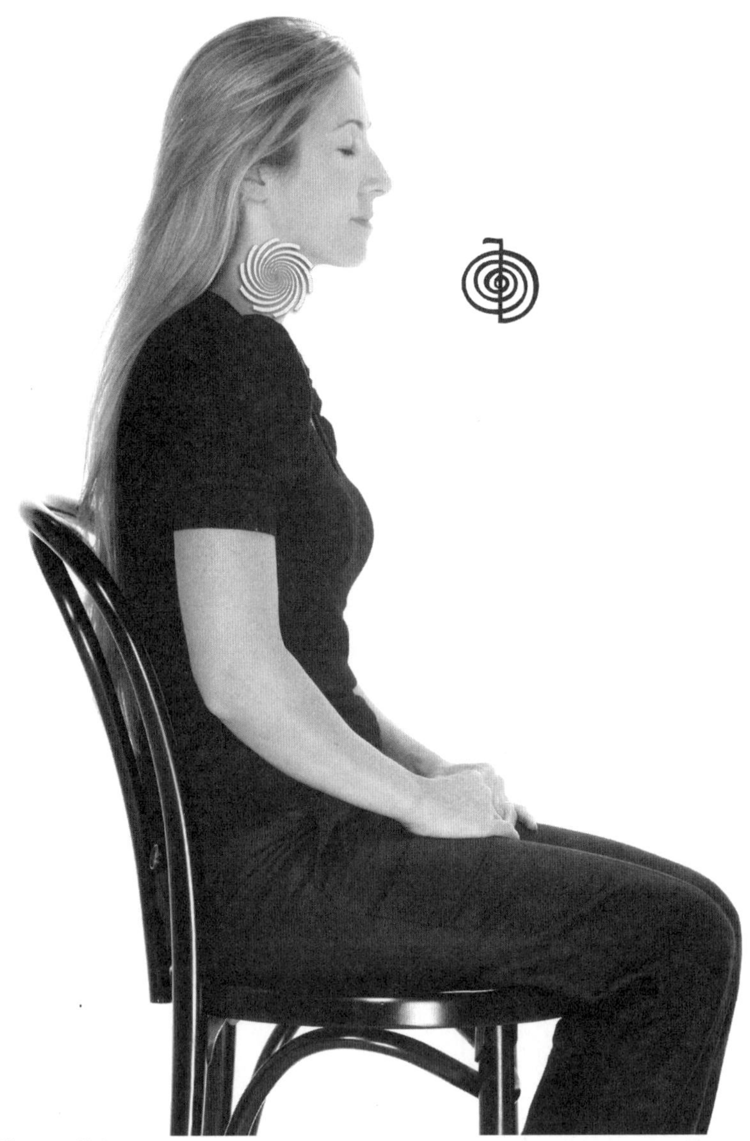

Photo 26

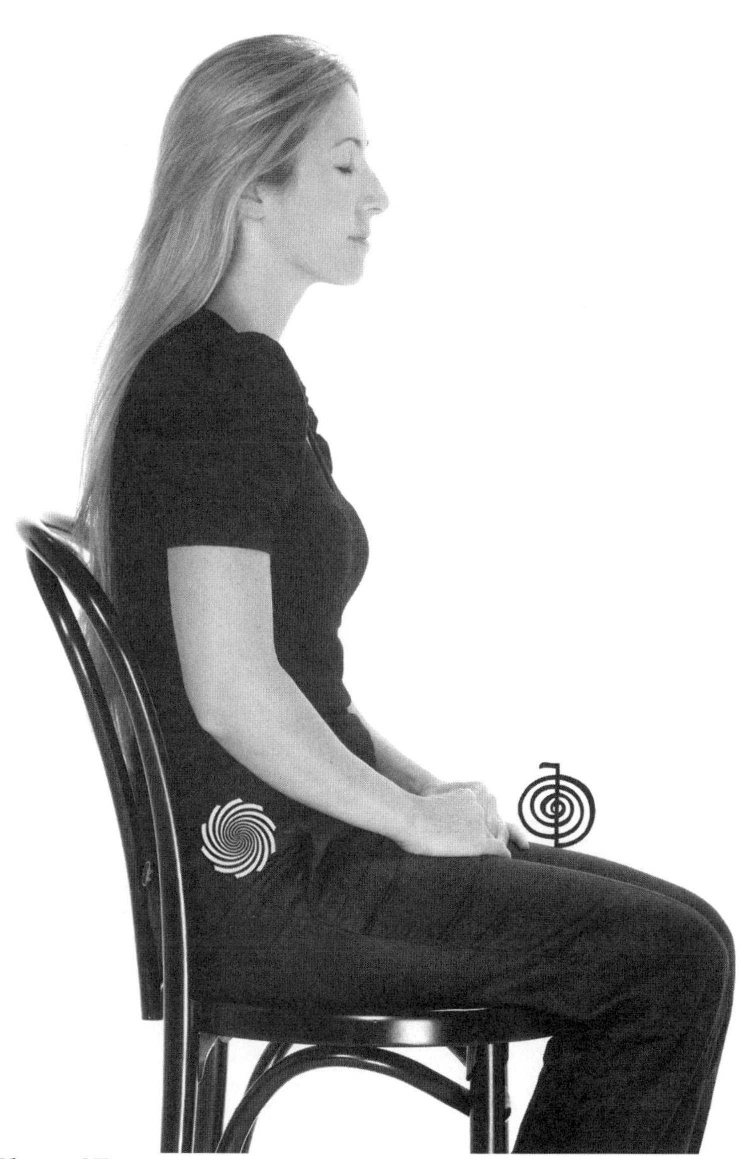

Photo 27

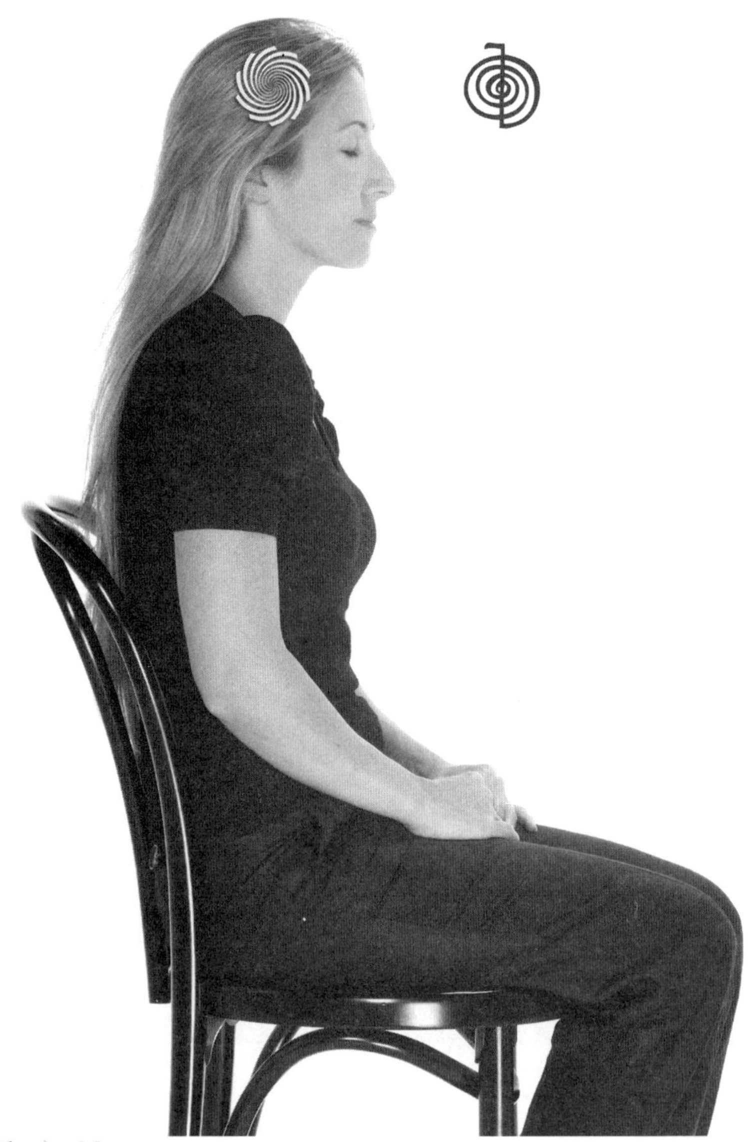

Photo 28

Photo 29

Often you have to rely on intuition.

- Bill Gates

Clairaudience Practice

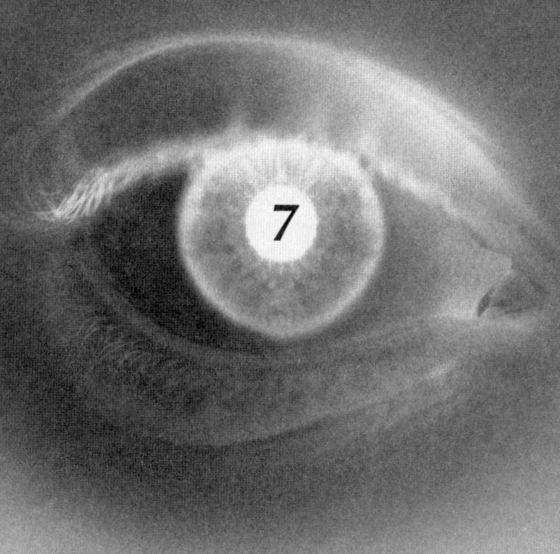

Practice

In this chapter there is a simple exercise you can practice after taking the Reiki Psychic Clairaudience Attunement. This exercise will help with expanding your Clairaudient ability, and at the same time you will able to monitor your progress.

Clairaudience Exercise

- Sit comfortably in a chair with a notebook and pen close by.
- Relax, close your eyes, and meditate for a few minutes.
- After a few minutes of meditation, state silently to yourself a question you know will be answered and verified within the next 48 hours.
- After asking the question, stay in the moment and be aware of what information you hear.
- Once you hear the information, write it down. Then verify what you heard with the outcome in the next few days.

If you do not hear information regarding your question within 10 minutes, stop the exercise and try again in a few days with another question. Even if you did not receive information during the exercise, you still might hear an answer in the next few days when you least expect it.

Don't be discouraged if you do not hear any information during the first few times you do this exercise. Just take the Clairaudience Attunement again after a few weeks and keep practicing this exercise. You will find your Clairaudient ability will expand with time and practice.

Clairsentience

You must train your intuition - you must trust the small voice inside you which tells you exactly what to say, what to decide.

- Ingrid Bergman

Clairsentience Review

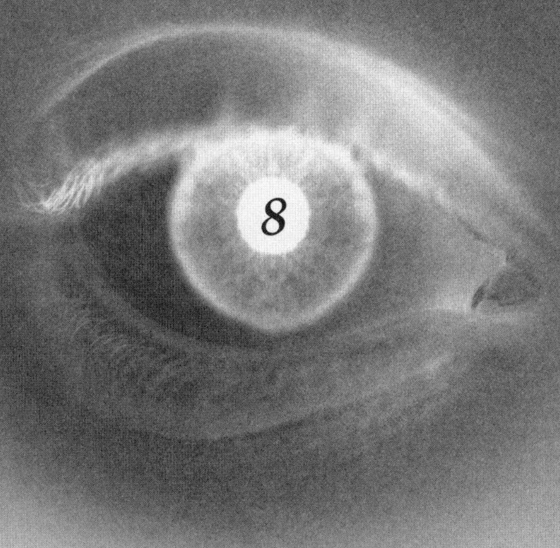

Clairsentience Defined

Clairsentience is known as "clear feeling," "clear sensing," or "inner knowing" and is associated with the Second Chakra. It is the psychic ability of receiving information through bodily sensations, gut feelings, hunches and sometimes smells.

Clairsentience Manifesting

This psychic ability expands your intuition. Intuition is usually experienced in the stomach region (Second Chakra) and this area will flutter, relax, or tighten when sensing and/or confirming Clairsentient information.

Individuals who have developed their Clairsentient ability to a high level are often called Empaths. Empaths have the ability to feel and sense how others feel on an emotional level and are powerful healers because they sense what type of healing is needed.

When they develop the ability of Clairsentience, some people are able to perceive the vibrations through the physical sensations of a person's Aura and by doing so can tell if the Aura is healthy. Or if they detect the Aura has rips or holes, they can commence with repairing and healing it.

The bottom line is when your Clairsentient ability is expanded, you can sense more of what you can't see, and you can understand more of what you feel. This will enable you to feel and/or sense if a person has any blockages in the mental, emotional or spiritual bodies that have already caused or will cause health challenges in the physical body in the future. Once this information is known, you can take the appropriate healing course of action to remove any blockage(s).

Follow your instincts. That's where true wisdom manifests itself.

- Oprah Winfrey

**Intuition is the clear conception
of the whole at once.**

- Johann Kaspar Lavater

Clairsentience Attunement

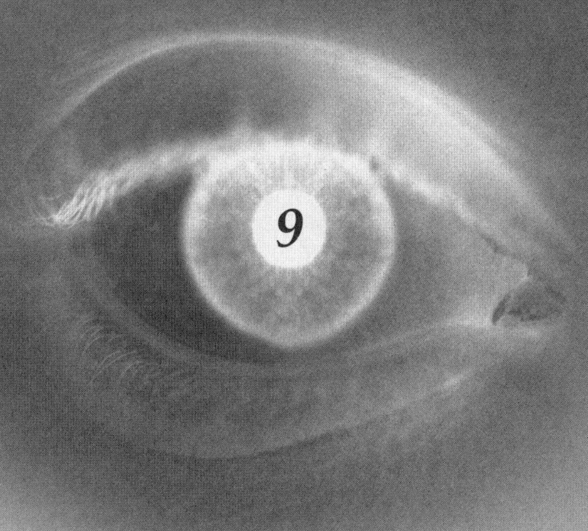

Giving the Clairsentience Attunement Step-by-Step

1. State a prayer and the intent for the attunement.

2. Place both of your hands over the Sixth Chakra for about a minute (Photo 30) with the intent to clear it.

Photo 30

From the Back

3. Draw or visualize Sei He Ki, the Emotional Symbol, over the Seventh Chakra (Photo 31), activate it and embed[8] the symbol into the Chakra.

4. Draw or visualize Dai Koo Myo, the Master Symbol, in front of the Second Chakra (Photo 32), activate it and embed the symbol into the Chakra.

5. Draw or visualize Hon Sha Ze Sho Nen, the Long Distance Symbol, in front of the Second Chakra (Photo 33), activate it and embed the symbol into the Chakra.

6. Draw or visualize the Emotional Symbol in front of the Second Chakra (Photo 34), activate it and embed the symbol into the Chakra.

7. Draw or visualize Cho Ku Rei, the Power Symbol, in front of the Third Chakra (Photo 35), activate it and embed the symbol into the Chakra.

8. Draw or visualize the Power Symbol in front of the Fourth Chakra (Photo 36), activate it and embed the symbol into the Chakra.

9. Channel Reiki into the Second Chakra for a few minutes (Photo 37).

---

[8] How to activate and embed Reiki Symbols are explained on pages 24 and 27.

Photo 31

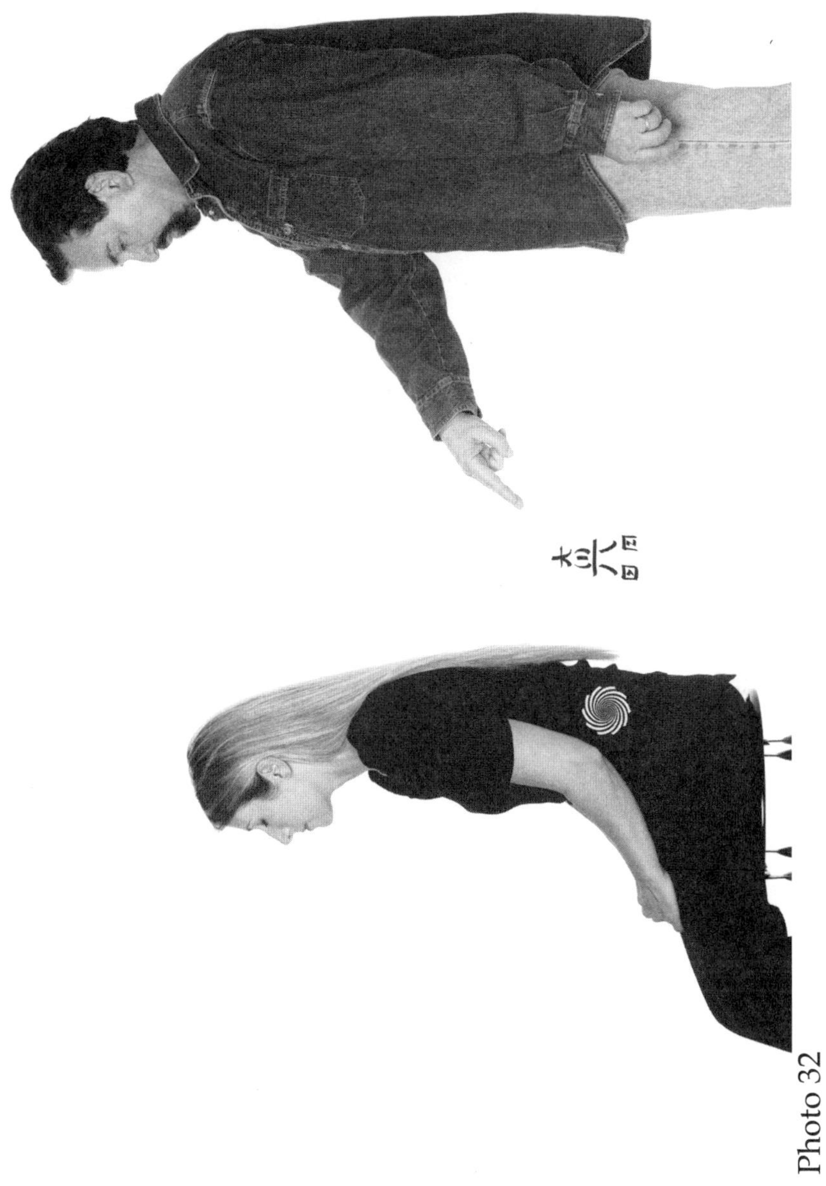

Photo 32

Photo 33

Photo 34

Photo 35

Photo 36

Photo 37

From the Front

10. Draw or visualize the Power Symbol in front of the Second Chakra (Photo 38), activate it and embed the symbol into the Chakra.

11. Draw or visualize the Power Symbol in front of the Third Chakra (Photo 39), activate it and embed the symbol into the Chakra.

12. Draw or visualize the Power Symbol in front of the Fourth Chakra (Photo 40), activate it and embed the symbol into the Chakra.

13. Channel Reiki into the Second Chakra for a few minutes (Photo 41).

14. Have the person receiving the attunement open their eyes (Photo 42), the attunement is complete.

Photo 38

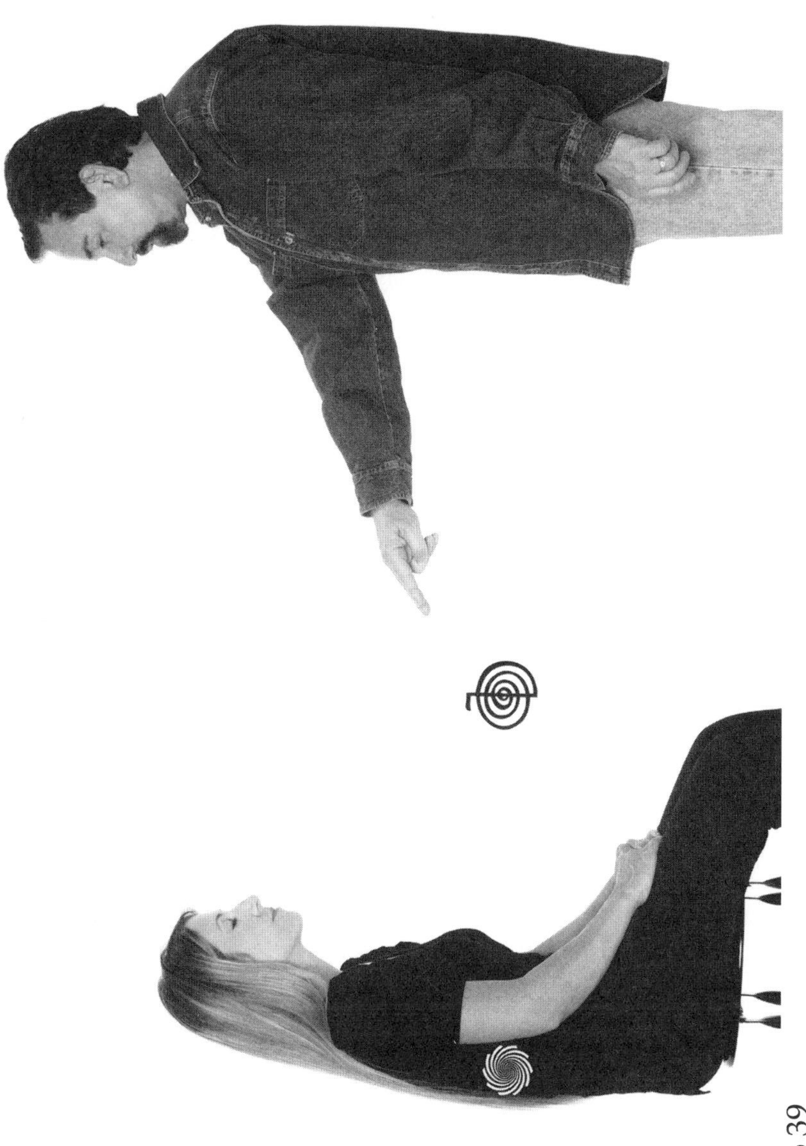

Photo 39

Photo 40

Photo 41

Photo 42

Clairsentience Self-Attunement Step-by-Step

1. State a prayer and the intent for the attunement.

2. Place a hand over the Sixth Chakra for about a minute (Photo 43) with the intent to clear it.

From the Back

3. Visualize Sei He Ki, the Emotional Symbol, over the Seventh Chakra (Photo 44), activate it and embed the symbol into the Chakra.

4. Visualize Dai Koo Myo, the Master Symbol, in front of the Second Chakra (Photo 45), activate it and embed the symbol into the Chakra.

5. Visualize Hon Sha Ze Sho Nen, the Long Distance Symbol, in front of the Second Chakra (Photo 46), activate it and embed the symbol into the Chakra.

6. Visualize the Emotional Symbol in front of the Second Chakra (Photo 47), activate it and embed the symbol into the Chakra.

7. Visualize Cho Ku Rei, the Power Symbol, in front of the Third Chakra (Photo 48), activate it and embed the symbol into the Chakra.

8. Visualize the Power Symbol in front of the Fourth Chakra (Photo 49), activate it and embed the symbol into the Chakra.

Photo 43

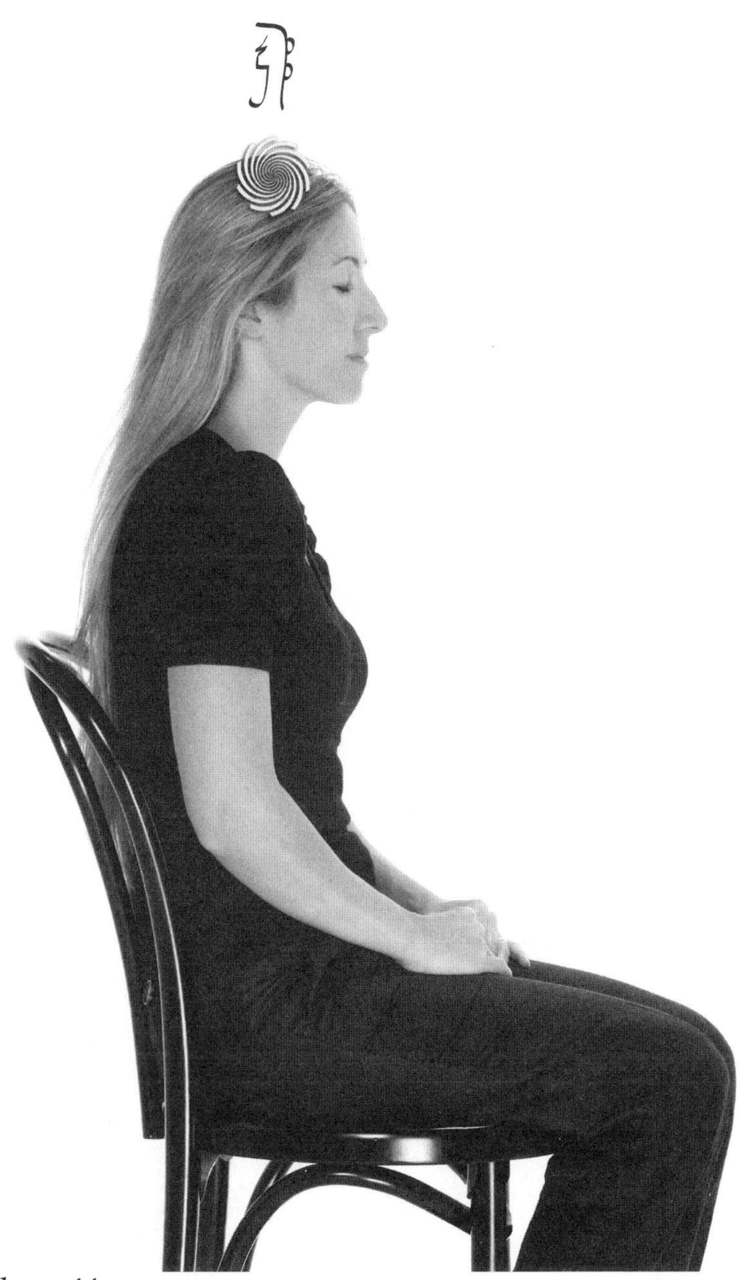

Photo 44

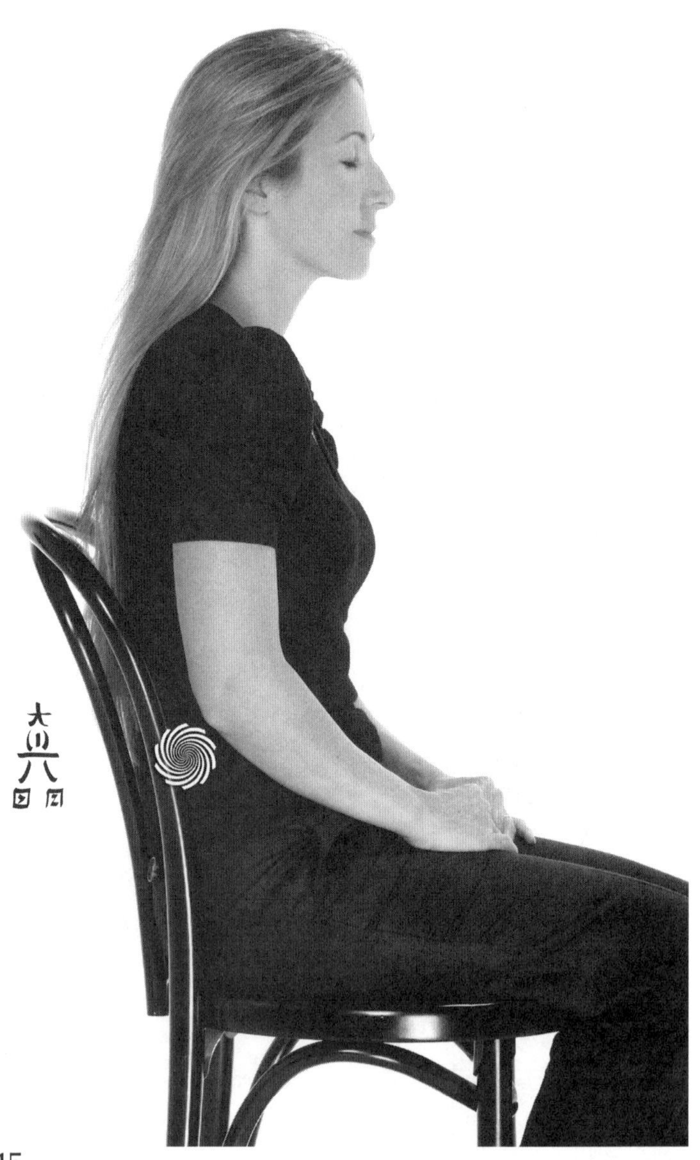

Photo 45

Photo 46

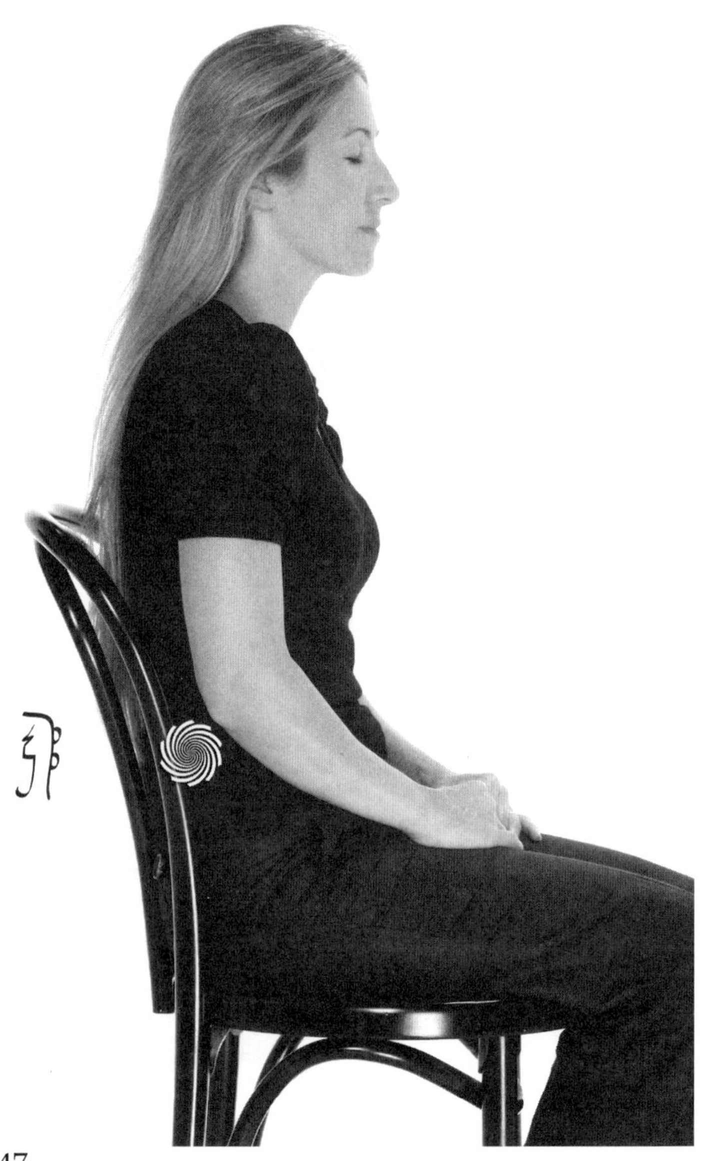

Photo 47

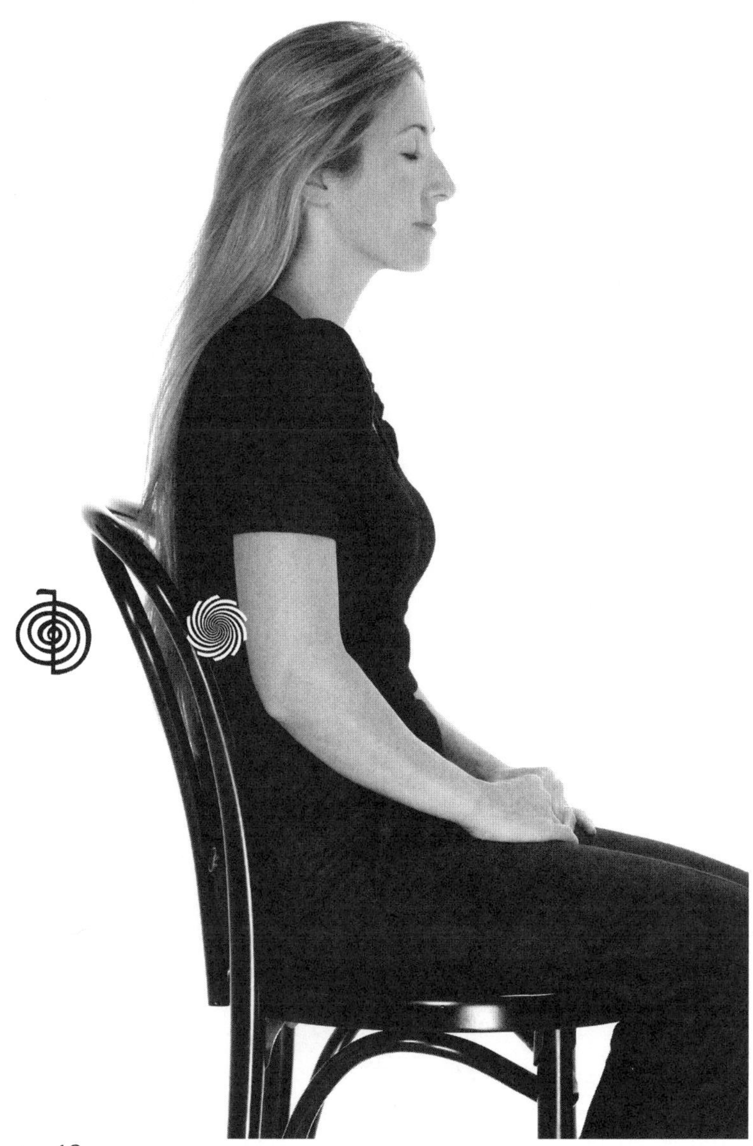

Photo 48

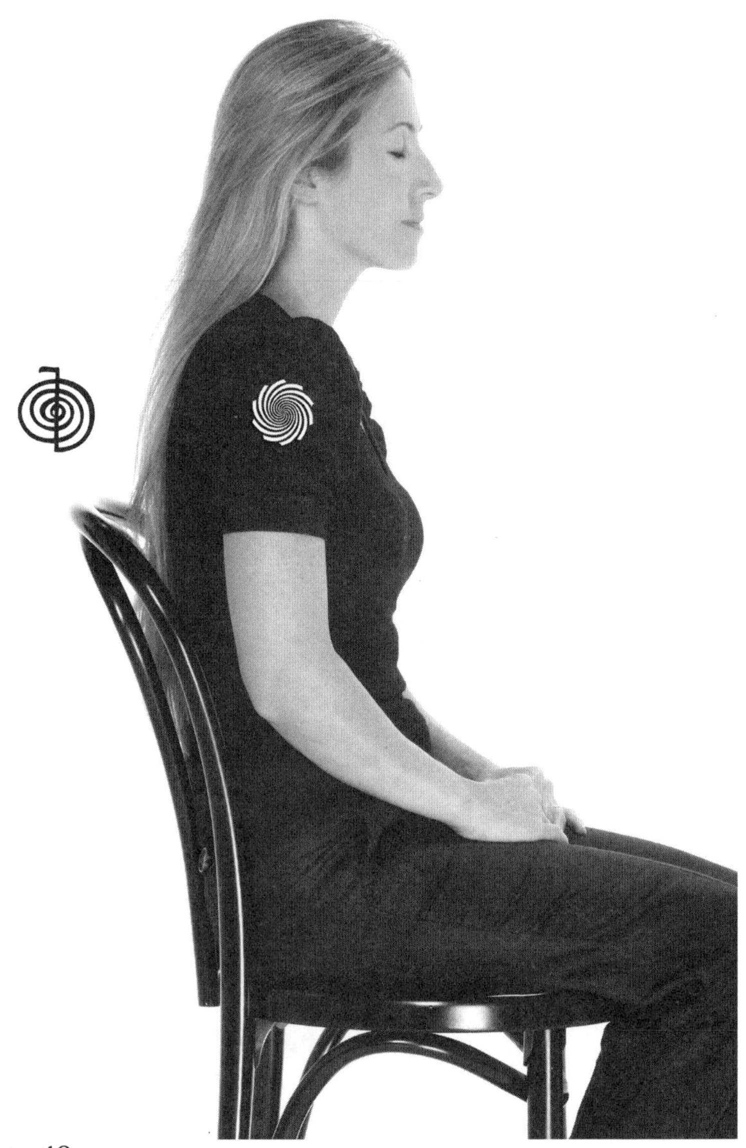

Photo 49

From the Front

9. Visualize the Power Symbol in front of the Second Chakra (Photo 50), activate it and embed the symbol into the Chakra.

10. Visualize the Power Symbol in front of the Third Chakra (Photo 51), activate it and embed the symbol into the Chakra.

11. Visualize the Power Symbol in front of the Fourth Chakra (Photo 52), activate it and embed the symbol into the Chakra.

12. Channel Reiki into the Second Chakra for a few minutes (Photo 53).

13. Open your eyes, the attunement is complete.

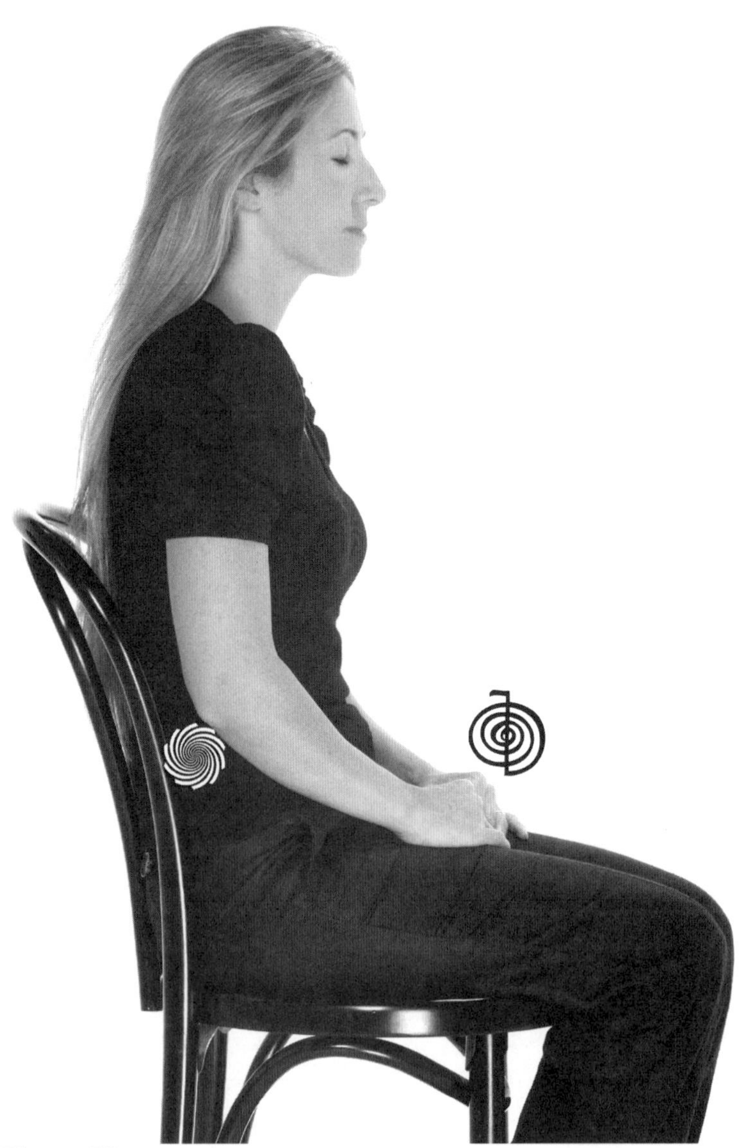

Photo 50

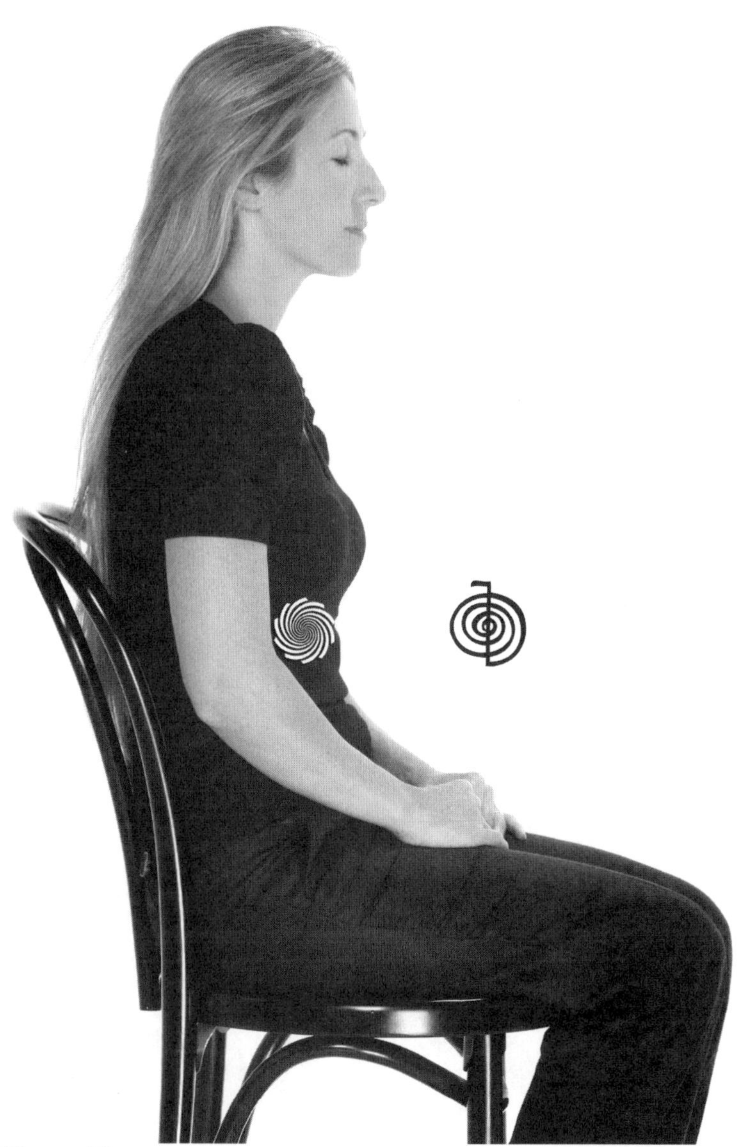

Photo 51

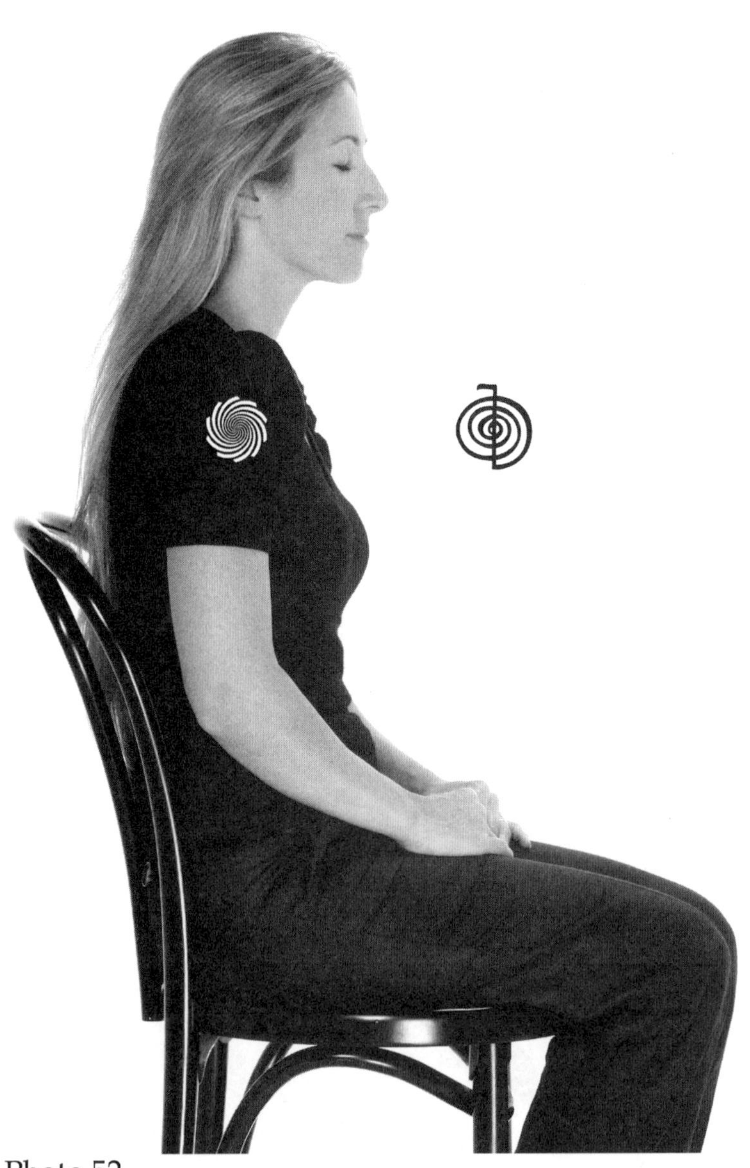

Photo 52

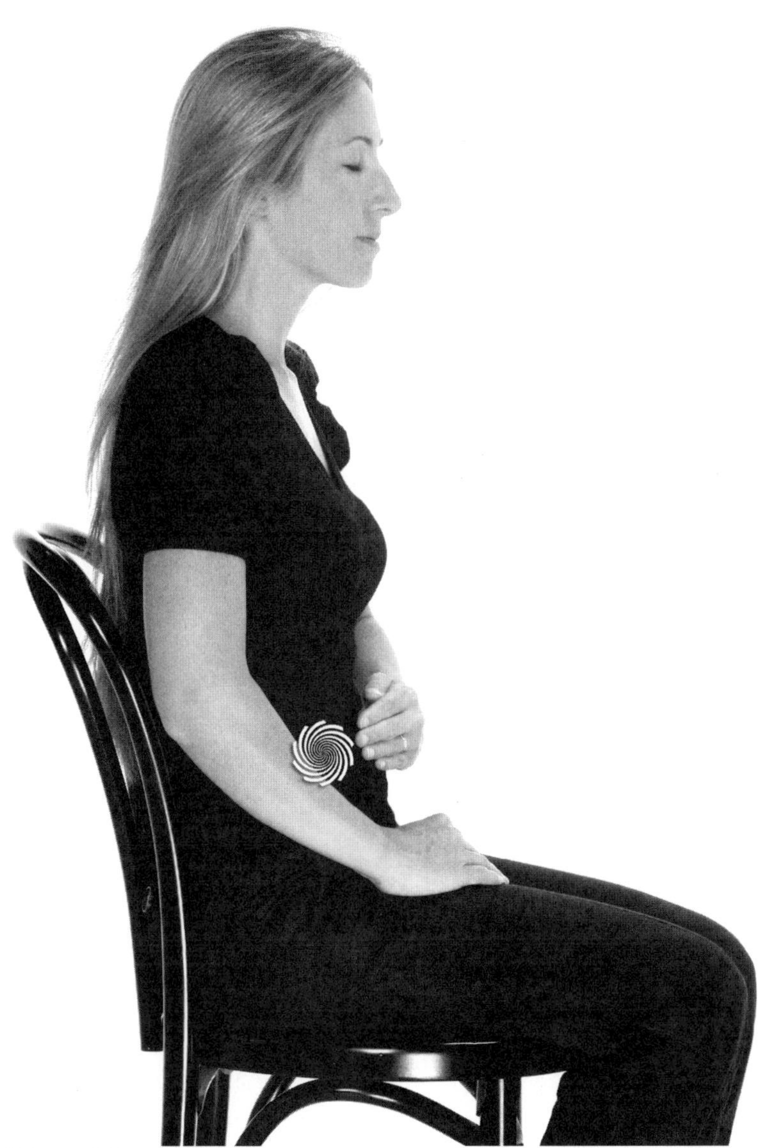

Photo 53

Trust yourself. You know more than you think you do.

- Benjamin Spock

Clairsentience Practice

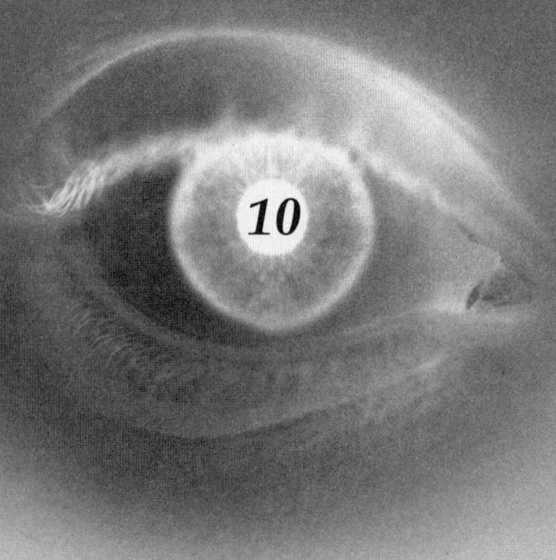

Practice

In this chapter there are several exercises you can practice after receiving the Reiki Psychic Clairsentience Attunement. These exercises will help with expanding your Clairsentient ability, and you will able to see the progress you are making on a daily basis.

Clairsentience Exercise # 1

- Choose a friend or a relative who you know will cooperate with you on this exercise, but do not tell them ahead of time.

- Sit comfortably in a chair with paper and pen close by. Write down the time of day on the paper and the person you selected for the exercise.

- Relax, close your eyes, and meditate for a few minutes.

- Now visualize and focus on the person you selected in your mind's eye, and feel or sense what the person is experiencing at this moment in time.

- After about five minutes, write down what you felt or sensed about the person whose name you wrote on the piece of paper.

- Call the person within the next 24 hours and ask what they were feeling and experiencing during the time you were doing the exercise. Then compare what they tell you with what you wrote.

If you do not receive information within five minutes, stop the exercise and try again within a few days. Always do this exercise with different friends and relatives to keep it interesting.

Clairsentience Exercise # 2

- For this exercise you will need a person in the same room with you. Have this person remember and visualize an event or a situation from their past. Have them really focus on it in detail for about five minutes.

- As the person is recalling the past memory, make sure your back is to the person so you are not picking up body language or facial expressions. After five minutes tell the person what you felt or sensed and see if you were correct or how close you came to sensing their feelings. You might also have received Clairvoyance and Clairaudience information during the five minutes. But the goal of the exercise is to sense what the person is feeling while recalling the memory, so focus on that. If you do receive information through another psychic ability, you can share that with the person after you have discussed the Clairsentience information.

Don't be discouraged if you do not feel or sense any psychic information doing one of the exercises the first few times. Just take the Clairsentience Attunement again after a few weeks and keep practicing both exercises. You will find your Clairsentient ability will expand and you will be successful with time and practice.

Intuition is a spiritual faculty
and does not explain,
but simply points the way.

- Florence Scovel Shinn

Clairvoyance

Listen to your intuition. It will tell you everything you need to know.

- Anthony J. D'Angelo

Clairvoyance Review

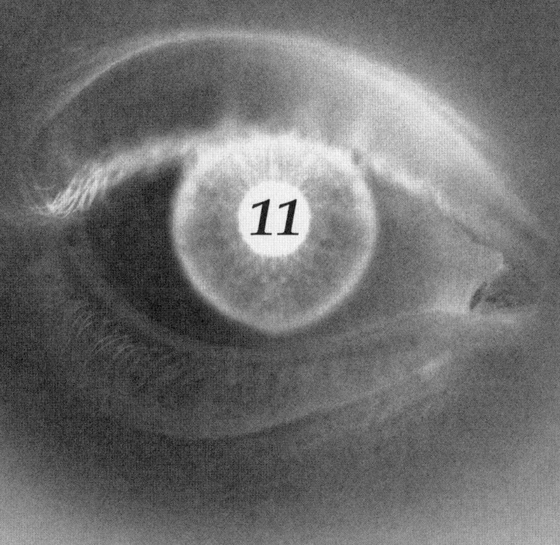

Clairvoyance Defined

Clairvoyance is the psychic ability referred to as "clear sight," "clear seeing," or second sight. It is associated with the Sixth Chakra, which is sometimes called the third eye or mind's eye. It is the psychic ability through which you can receive information in pictures, images, visions, colors, symbols, and the Aura. This information can be received through the mind's eye, dreams, or outside the physical body. If the psychic information is received in images or pictures, they can be either black and white or in color. The images and pictures may appear like a brief flash or snapshot or they can be a rapid series of images or pictures, much like a movie.

This psychic ability is extremely helpful in healing. When expanded, not only will this ability let you see the root cause of an illness and where it has manifested, it can also let you see the best healing option to use.

Clairvoyance should not be mistaken for telepathy, which is reading a person's mind.

Aura Colors

When the ability of Clairvoyance is expanded, besides receiving psychic information via images, picture, visions, etc., very often you can see the Aura and its colors around yourself and others. By viewing the Aura's colors, you can learn to interpret colors that represent blockages that can create health problems, and then perform the healing to remove the blockages. Or if a physical illness has already manifested, you can tell by the color in the Aura where the problem is located and what is causing the physical challenge. Then you can perform what you feel is needed to heal that part of the Aura.

The intuition of free will gives us the truth.
- Corliss Lamont

I allow my intuition to lead my path.

- Manuel Puig

Clairvoyance Attunement

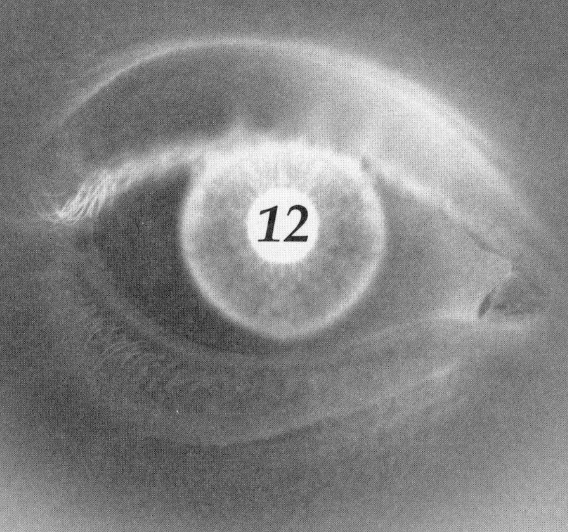

Giving the Clairvoyance Attunement Step-by-Step

1. State a prayer and intent for the attunement.

2. Place both of your hands over the Sixth Chakra (Photo 54) for about a minute with the intent to clear it.

Photo 54

From the Back

3. Draw or visualize Sei He Ki, the Emotional Symbol, over the Seventh Chakra (Photo 55), activate it and embed[9] the symbol into the Chakra.

4. Draw or visualize Dai Koo Myo, the Master Symbol, in front of the Sixth Chakra (Photo 56), activate it and embed the symbol into the Chakra.

5. Draw or visualize Hon Sha Ze Sho Nen, the Long Distance Symbol, in front of the Sixth Chakra (Photo 57), activate it and embed the symbol into the Chakra.

6. Draw or visualize the Emotional Symbol in front of the Sixth Chakra (Photo 58), activate it and embed the symbol into the Chakra.

7. Draw or visualize Cho Ku Rei, the Power Symbol, in front of the Fourth Chakra (Photo 59), activate it and embed the symbol into the Chakra.

8. Draw or visualize the Power Symbol in front of the Second Chakra (Photo 60), activate it and embed the symbol into the Chakra.

9. Channel Reiki into the Sixth Chakra (Photo 61) for a few minutes.

---

[9] How to activate and embed Reiki Symbols are explained on pages 24 and 27.

Photo 55

Photo 56

Photo 57

Photo 58

Photo 59

Photo 60

Photo 61

From the Front

10. Draw or visualize the Power Symbol in front of the Sixth Chakra (Photo 62), activate it and embed the symbol into the Chakra.

11. Draw or visualize the Power Symbol in front of the Fourth Chakra (Photo 63), activate it and embed the symbol into the Chakra.

12. Draw or visualize the Power Symbol in front of the Second Chakra (Photo 64), activate it and embed the symbol into the Chakra.

13. Channel Reiki into the Sixth Chakra (Photo 65) for a few minutes.

14. Have the person open their eyes (Photo 66), the attunement is complete.

Photo 62

Photo 63

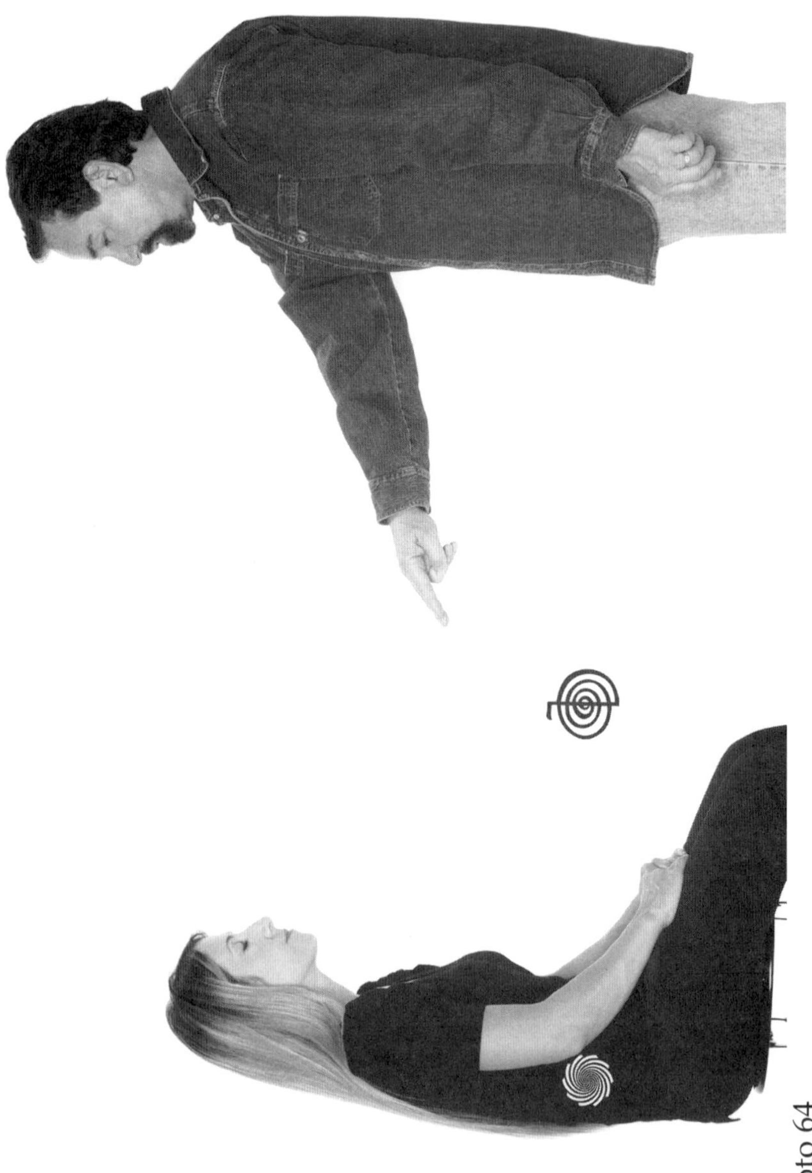

Photo 64

Photo 65

Photo 66

Clairvoyance Self-Attunement Step-by-Step

1. State a prayer and intent for the attunement.

2. Place a hand over the Sixth Chakra (Photo 67) for about a minute with the intent to clear it.

From the Back

3. Visualize Sei He Ki, the Emotional Symbol, over the Seventh Chakra (Photo 68), activate it and embed the symbol into the Chakra.

4. Visualize Dai Koo Myo, the Master Symbol, in front of the Sixth Chakra (Photo 69), activate it and embed the symbol into the Chakra.

5. Visualize Hon Sha Ze Sho Nen, the Long Distance Symbol, in front of the Sixth Chakra (Photo 70), activate it and embed the symbol into the Chakra.

6. Visualize the Emotional Symbol in front of the Sixth Chakra (Photo 71), activate it and embed the symbol into the Chakra.

7. Visualize Cho Ku Rei, the Power Symbol, in front of the Fourth Chakra (Photo 72), activate it and embed the symbol into the Chakra.

8. Visualize the Power Symbol in front of the Second Chakra (Photo 73), activate it and embed the symbol into the Chakra.

Photo 67

Photo 68

Photo 69

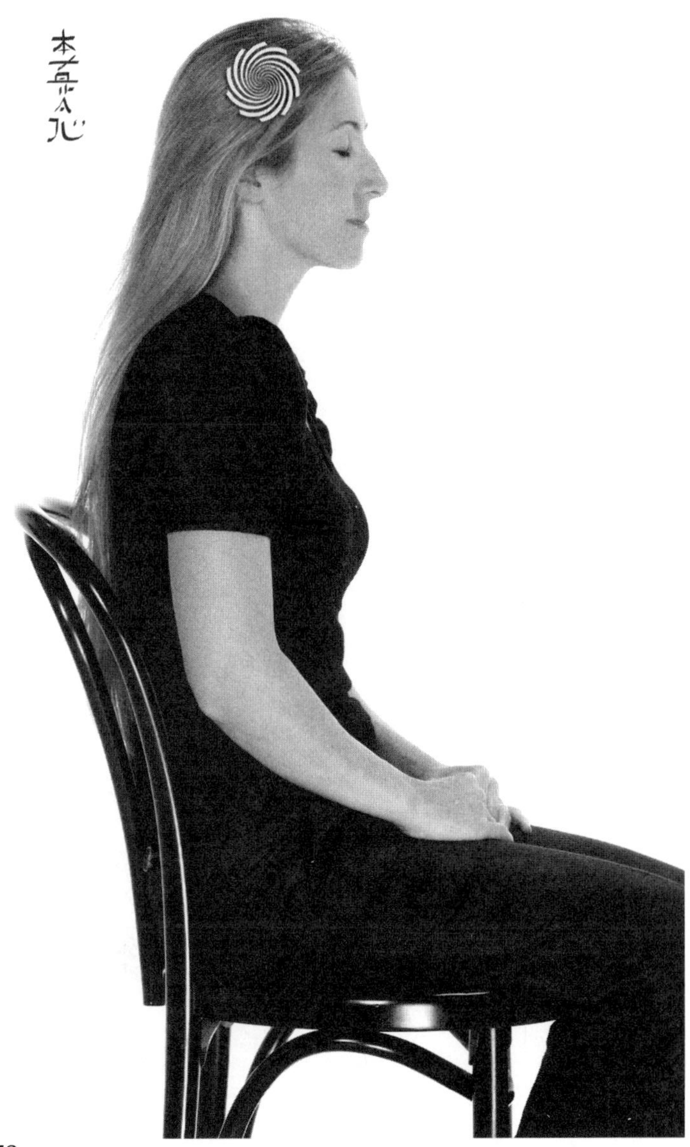

Photo 70

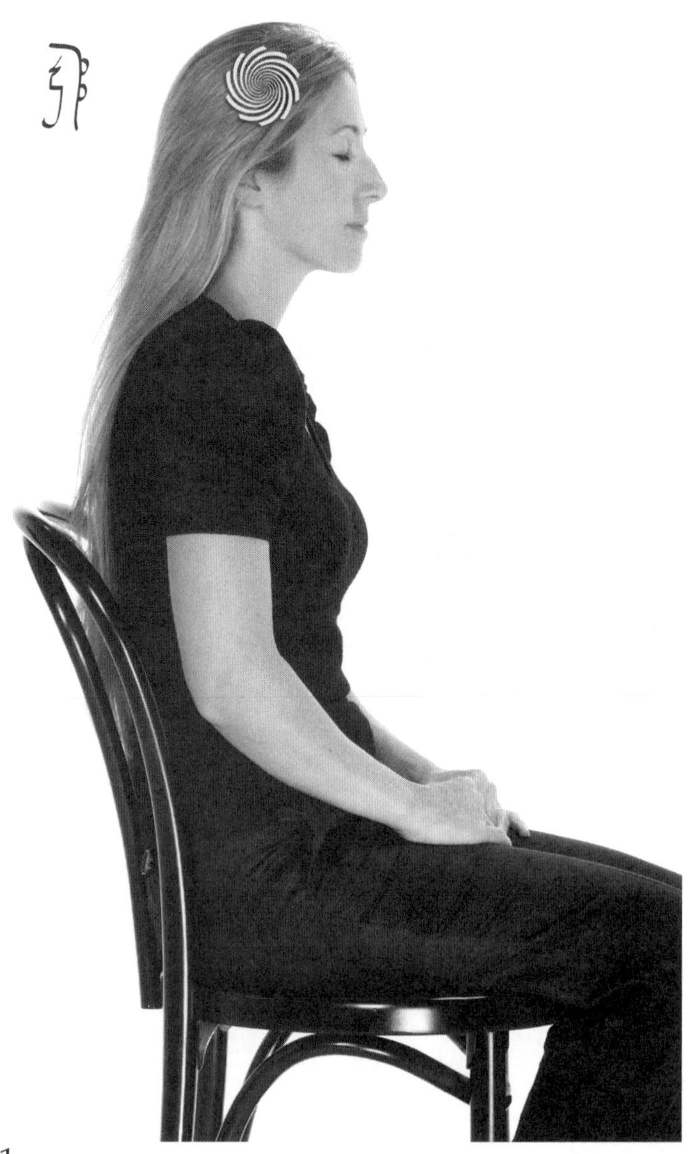

Photo 71

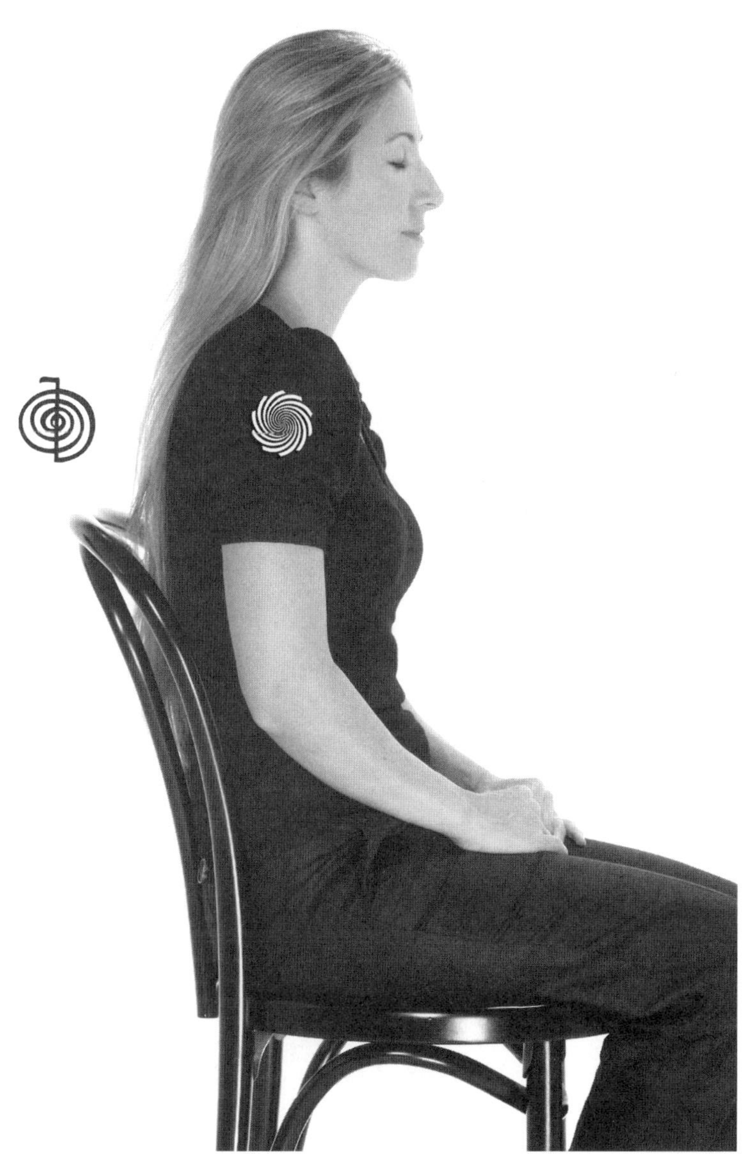

Photo 72

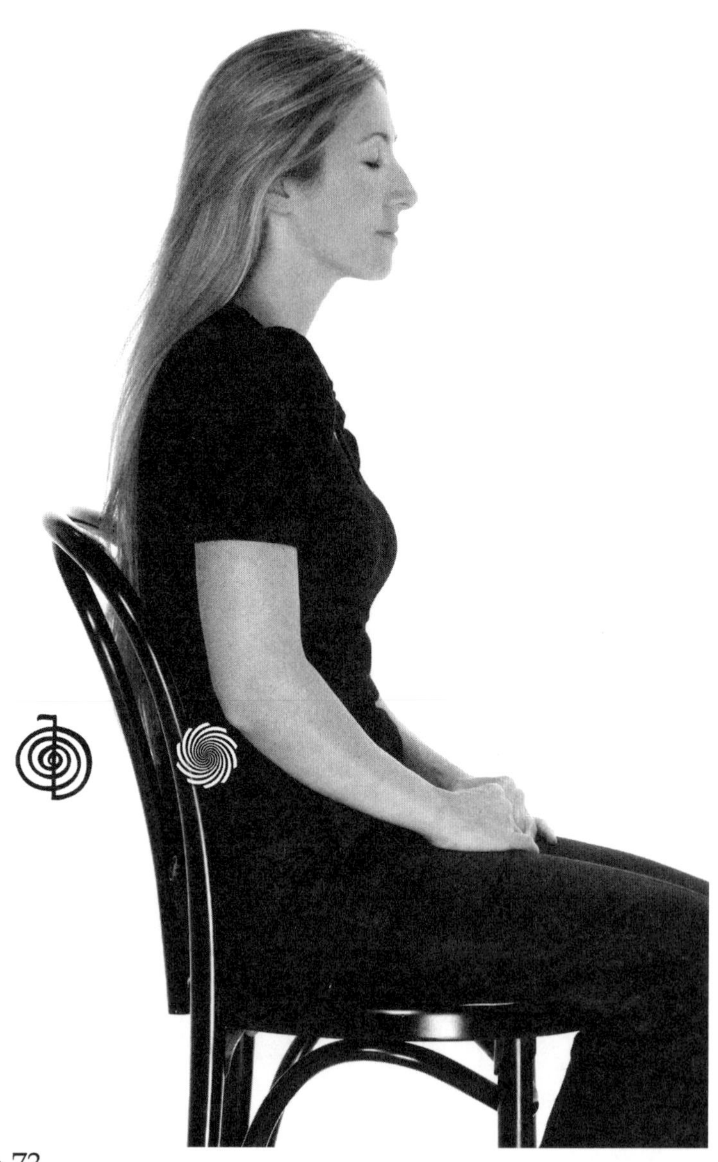

Photo 73

From the Front

9. Visualize the Power Symbol in front of the Sixth Chakra (Photo 74), activate it and embed the symbol into the Chakra.

10. Visualize the Power Symbol in front of the Fourth Chakra (Photo 75), activate it and embed the symbol into the Chakra.

11. Visualize the Power Symbol in front of the Second Chakra (Photo 76), activate it and embed the symbol into the Chakra.

12. Channel Reiki into the Sixth Chakra (Photo 77) for a few minutes.

13. Open your eyes, the attunement is complete.

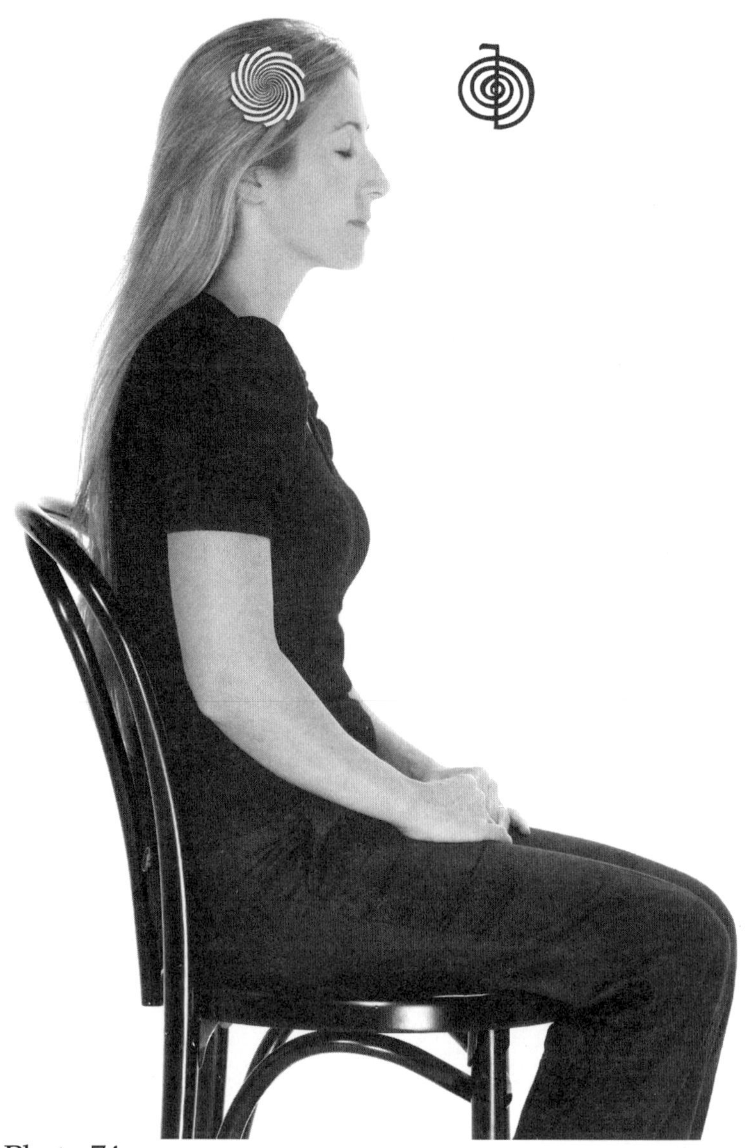

Photo 74

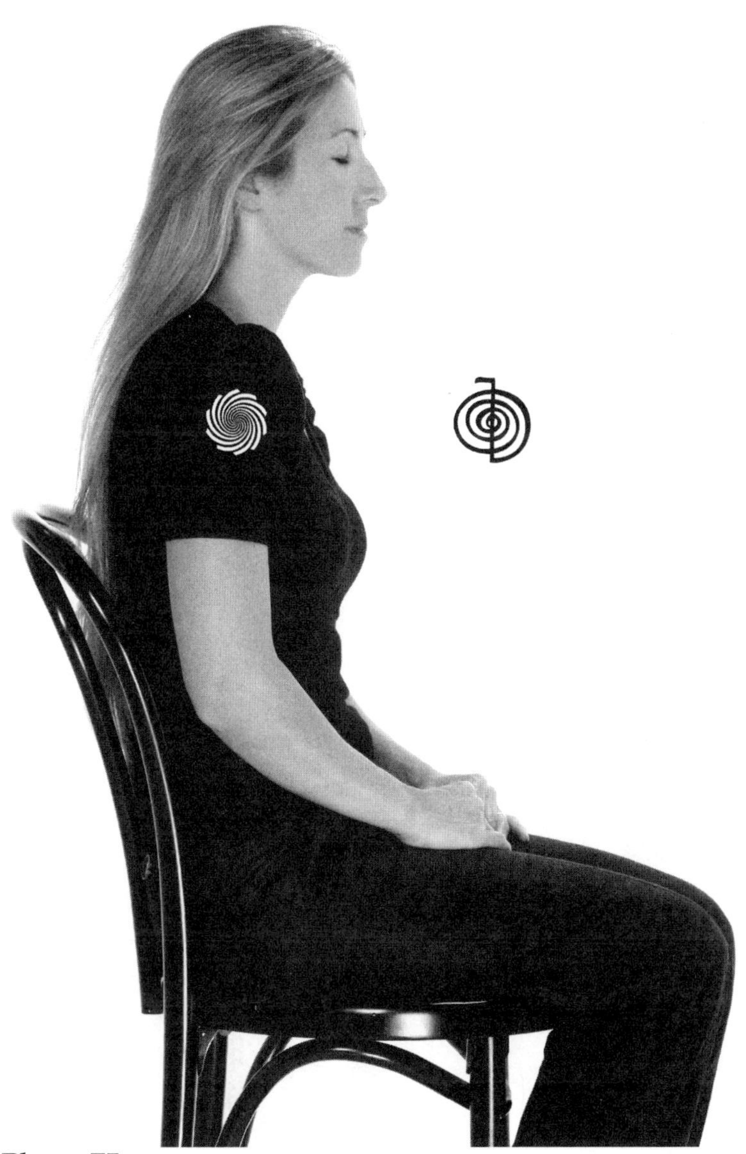

Photo 75

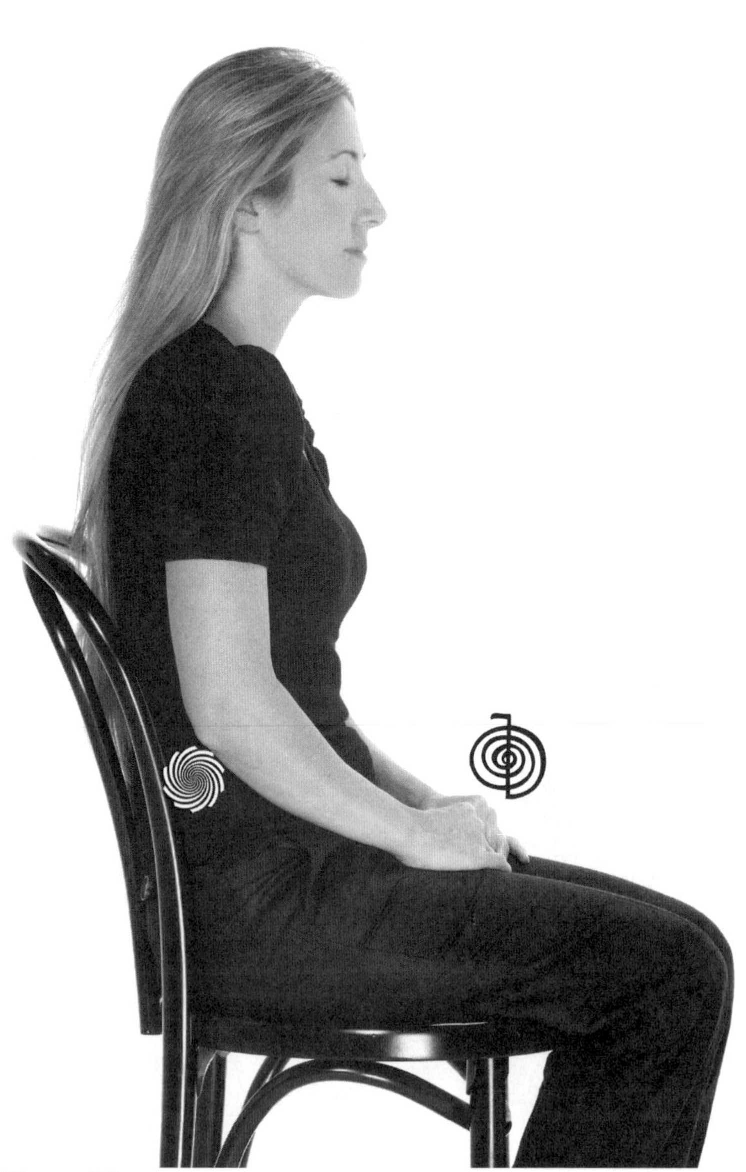

Photo 76

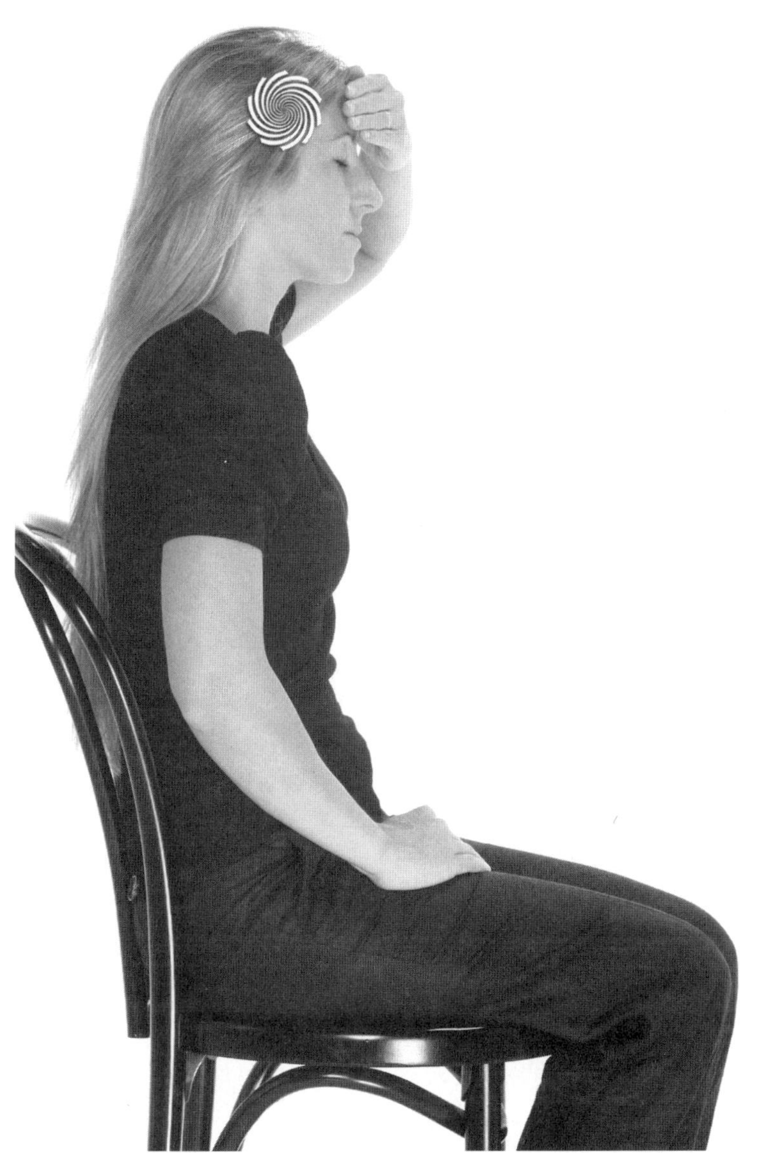

Photo 77

Trusting our intuition often saves us from disaster.

- Anne Wilson Schaef

Clairvoyance Practice

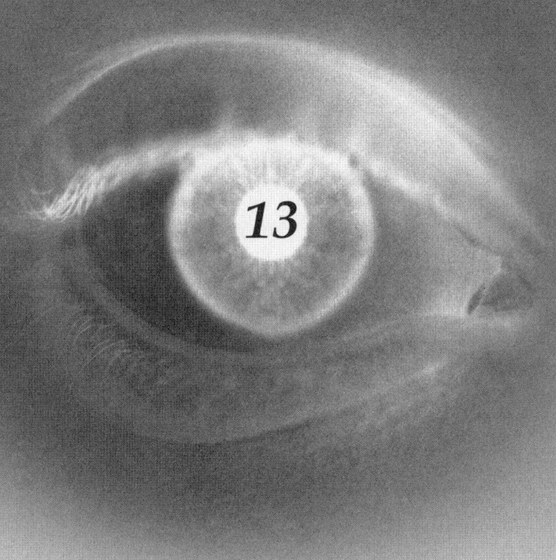

Practice

In this chapter is a well known Clairvoyance exercise that can be modified to make it more challenging as you progress. The results of this exercise also make it very easy to keep comparing day to day to see how much you are expanding your Clairvoyant ability.

Clairvoyance Exercise

- For this exercise you will need a standard fifty-two deck of playing cards. A standard playing deck has four symbols, Heart, Spade, Diamond, and Club. Each symbol is on 13 cards.

- Have a piece of paper and pen near by. On the paper draw two columns: one labeled "yes" and one labeled "no." Shuffle the cards and place them face down on the table in front of you.

- Now focus on the top card of the deck and its symbol. Your eyes can be closed or opened for this. Once you see a symbol in your mind's eye, turn the card over to see if you are correct. If you do not see a symbol within 5-10 seconds, turn the card over and count that as a "no" (see next step) and move to the next card.

- If the symbol you saw in your mind's eye is correct, place a mark in the "yes" column, if not, place a mark in the "no" column.

- Go through the entire deck seeing in your mind's eye what the symbol on the top card is and then making note of whether or not you were correct.

- The first time you do the exercise, the total number of "yes" answers are your benchmark for the exercise. As your Clairvoyance expands, the number of correct calls of the card's suit will also go up, surpassing this benchmark. This will help give you confidence in your Clairvoyance ability and give you an easy way to track your progress.

- When you name thirteen or more correct symbols in a practice session you really are starting to expand your Clairvoyant abilities.

Don't be discouraged if the first few times you don't name a high percentage of symbols correctly. Keep practicing this exercise, and you will expand your Clairvoyance.

Once you have mastered this exercise, you can modify it and take it to a higher level by naming the card and even naming the card and symbol. You can also use a tarot deck[10] for this exercise as you progress which will make it even more challenging.

[10] Most Tarot decks have 78 cards and have four symbols: Wands, Pentacles, Swords and Cups. Each symbol is on 14 cards, with 22 additional Major Arcana cards.

My gut and intuition told me it wasn't time to do this.

- Mario Vazquez

Psychic Cords

When luck runs out, sense runs in.

- Joshua Montenegro

Psychic Cords Overview

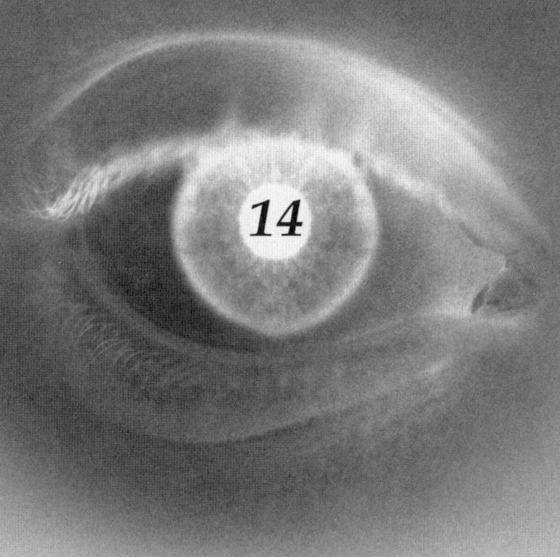

Psychic Cords

Psychic Cords are energetic attachments that are connected between two individuals' corresponding Chakras. They are formed and connected consciously or unconsciously by both parties, and they are connected over time and space, even after death.

The cords are invisible to most people, but those who can see them describe Psychic Cords as rubbery, dense, and sometimes glowing flexible lines that extend from a Chakra.

There are two types of Psychic Cords, positive and negative. Most Psychic Cords are first formed as a positive cord and can remain that way for a lifetime, or until they are disconnected or go dormant. When a Psychic Cord forms as a negative cord or a positive cord turns into a negative cord, it can cause health problems. We all have Psychic Cords, but regrettably, some are not positive.

Creating a Psychic Cord

A positive Psychic Cord manifests anytime two people agree, whether consciously or unconsciously to connect to each other for emotional and/or energetic support. Once connected, the cord is a direct pipeline through each person's Aura and a corresponding Chakra[11]. This makes it easy to share emotional information and energy between both people when it is needed, by one or the other. Psychic Cords most typically are formed between children, parents, spouses, sexual partners, siblings, friends or co-workers.
When a positive cord is formed, it is always a balanced, healthy situation, even though one person is receiving and the other is usually giving emotional or energetic support through the cord. There are unlimited reasons and circumstances why a positive Psychic Cord is formed

[11] The Chakra through which two people will be connected depends on the reasons for the connection, e.g., lovers may be connected by a Psychic Cord from their Fourth Chakras, also known as the Heart Chakra.

between two people. The strongest positive Psychic Cords are those that are created in intimate, stressful or traumatic moments. Here are a few examples of positive Psychic Cords:

- Two lovers who have a cord from Heart Chakra to Heart Chakra.

- A husband and a wife. The husband has a kidney problem. A Psychic Cord is connected between their Third Chakras' area of influence (where the kidneys are located.)

- Two co-workers working together on a stressful project. A psychic cord is connected between their Sixth Chakras.

- Siblings' (brother-brother, brother-sister, sister-sister) Psychic Cords are connected from Heart Chakra to Heart Chakra.

The majority of time a positive Psychic Cord will naturally disconnect by itself or go dormant once it is consciously or unconsciously agreed by both parties that it is no longer needed. The problem is when a positive Psychic Cord has run its course and in reality it is not needed by both parties. And unfortunately the cord remains connected because, consciously or unconsciously, one party will not disconnect for various reasons depending on their circumstances. This becomes an extremely unbalanced and unhealthy situation for the one party that is willing to disconnect. This once positive cord is now a negative cord. Here are few examples of a positive Psychic Cord forming and then changing to a negative Psychic Cord:

- A couple marries, 15 years later they divorce. One person does not want the divorce and refuses to let go.

- A couple is dating. One person breaks up, the other person wants to continue dating.

- A mentor in any type of relationship is no longer needed, but wants to continue mentoring.

- Any type of positive relationship, business or personal, that started out beneficial for both parties comes to an end. One party refuses to move on.

A Psychic Cord can be formed as a negative cord from the start. Again, both parties have to agree on a conscious or unconscious level for the negative cord to manifest. There are many reasons and circumstances why the person who will be suffering from this cord connection will consent to the attachment. It can range from guilt, low self-esteem, and self-punishment to a perceived need from the other person. It can also be one person in a power play or controlling situation over the other. Every negative cord is unique as to why it was formed. Here are a few examples of circumstances where a negative Psychic Cord could form:

- An abusive parent and child

- An alcoholic and a loved one

- An abusive husband and wife

- An authoritarian boss and employee

Over time, a negative Psychic Cord weakens your immune system due to emotional and energetic draining. This can manifest minor, chronic, or severe problems on mental, emotional, spiritual and/or physical levels. And, the symptoms can vary greatly with each person.

Once a negative Psychic Cord is disconnected, the channel from Chakra to Chakra is no longer available for a continuous emotion or energy drain. Your life becomes whole and balanced, symptoms from the negative connection will disappear, and you can start healing.

Discovering a Cord

You will always sense or suspect it if you have a negative Psychic Cord attachment with a person. The signs of a negative cord attachment are feelings of being emotionally and/or physically drained after having any type of contact or just thinking of the person in question. And these signs will have been happening over an extended period of time. Now these signs that I've just described can occur over a short period of time with any person in your life as a result of circumstances created by everyday living, but they are always temporary. The signs of a negative Psychic Cord that I'm talking about are when a person feels continually drained, emotionally and/or physically, by another person over an extended, ongoing period of time. Here's a simple two-part test to verify that there is a probability you have a negative Psychic Cord with another person.

1. First close your eyes and relax for a few moments. Then think of or visualize the person with whom you suspect there is a negative cord attachment and the circumstances of the last time you had contact. After a few moments of recalling the last interaction you had with this person, how do you feel? Do you feel drained mentally or physically? Or perhaps you feel stress or experience negative emotions? If the answer is "yes," do the second part.

2. Now ask yourself,"What I'm experiencing with this recalled memory, has it been happening over an extended period of time with this person?" If the answer is "yes" there's a strong possibility you have a negative Psychic Cord connection. The reason I say there is only a possibility is that you really don't actually know if, in fact, there is a negative cord with this person until you have a negative Psychic Cord disconnect session. But, if the answer is "yes" and "yes" on the test, I strongly recommend doing a session to find out if indeed there is a negative cord with this person. And if so, disconnect the cord during the session.

Chakra Protection

When you disconnect a negative Psychic Cord, it is likely the other person to whom it was attached will contact you in an attempt to reconnect the cord. He or she will know, either on a conscious or unconscious level, that the negative Psychic Cord is no longer connected. The ideal situation would be to break off all contact with that person, but in real life, this is not always possible (i.e., the person could be a relative, neighbor, boss, etc.) So, when you are in communication with this person, you need to protect your Chakra that was previously connected to theirs. Here are a few options[12] for protecting your Chakra when the situation arises.

- Visualize a golden or white light vibrating Psychic Shield covering the Chakra.
- Visualize a golden or white light solid orb spinning fast over the Chakra.
- Visualize a highly polished mirror reflecting outward from and covering the Chakra.
- If you feel the need to protect all your Chakras, then visualize your whole body encased in a bubble of golden or white light.

The good news is that you do not have to know why you permitted a negative cord to attach in order to disconnect it, and you can disconnect a positive cord that has become a negative cord. In the next chapter, I'll show you how.

[12] You can also search the Internet or your local library for other options. I also list a few books on Chakras in the bibliography on page 217.

When our knowing exceeds our sensing,
we will no longer be deceived
by the illusions of our senses.

- Walter Russell

Disconnect Psychic Cords

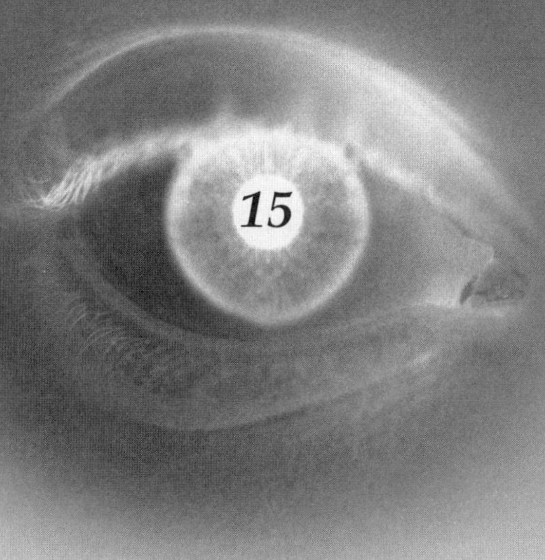

Six Issues

This Chapter will show you how to perform a negative Psychic Cord disconnect session for yourself and how to guide another person through one. Before we get into the instruction, there are six issues regarding negative Psychic Cords that you should know.

Negative Psychic Cord Issues

- You do not need to know the reason why a negative Psychic Cord was formed with another person to successfully disconnect it.

- A negative cord can be reconnected if you do not protect your Chakra as described in the previous chapter. If that does happen, just perform another disconnect session.

- You can have negative cords with more than one person. If you find this is the case, perform only one disconnect session at a time (that is, disconnect only one person per session.)

- You can have a positive and a negative Psychic Cord with the same person, and you would only want to disconnect the negative one.

- You will always be able to tell the difference between positive cords and negative cords by the color. Positive cords are always gold or white. Negative cords are never gold or white; they are different colors, usually dark colors like black or grey.

- Before you perform a negative Psychic Cord disconnect session, I recommend taking all three of the Psychic Attunements in this book first. This will help in all facets of a disconnect session.

A Negative Psychic Cord Disconnect Session Step-By-Step

1. Sit in a room where you will not be disturbed for at least 30 minutes.

2. Ask your Source, Higher Power, Universal Mind, Spirit Guide, Guardian Angel, etc., to help reveal to you any negative Psychic Cord attachments during the disconnect session.

3. Now meditate or get into a relaxed state for five minutes.

4. Next, visualize the individual that you suspect you have a negative cord with and see if there is a cord extending from a Chakra (Photo 78, Heart Chakra is used as an example) of this person connecting to one of your Chakras. If there is a cord, what color is it and to which one of your Chakras is it connected? If you do not see a cord and/or if the cord you see is white or gold, then take a few deep breaths and end the session.

5. If you have not ended the session, this means you have a negative Psychic Cord attachment to this person and you know to which of your Chakras it is connected.

6. Now, speak to this person mentally (speaking aloud if you wish) and tell them that you intend to disconnect the negative Psychic Cord attachment that exists between the two of you. This is also the time to release any anger or grudges, if you have any towards that person. As an option, some people feel the need to say

Photo 78

more before they disconnect the cord, though it is not necessary, it is okay. For example, you might tell the person that you are sorry for all of the things you said or did that hurt him/her. Or, you may wish to forgive him/her for all the hurtful things that were said or done in the relationship. Once you have done this, move to the next step.

7. Next with strong, focused, conscious intent, visualize, know or imagine the negative cord connection to your Chakra being dissolved with white or golden light (Photo 79). Now do the same (Photo 80) for the person you have visualized. Do not worry about the remainder of the cord; once it is disconnected it will start to dissolve instantly by itself because there is not a dual connection to sustain it.

8. Where the negative cord was connected in your Chakra, there is now a hole, a void. First, visualize filling this void with white or golden light, then embed (Photo 81) the Reiki Emotional Symbol into it. Now do the same (Photo 82) for the person you visualized.

9. After Step #8 is complete, channel Reiki for a few minutes into your Chakra (Photo 83, Heart Chakra is used as an example) that is now free of the negative Psychic Cord attachment.

10. When you are done channeling the Reiki, take several deep breaths and open your eyes; the session is over.

Photo 79

Photo 80

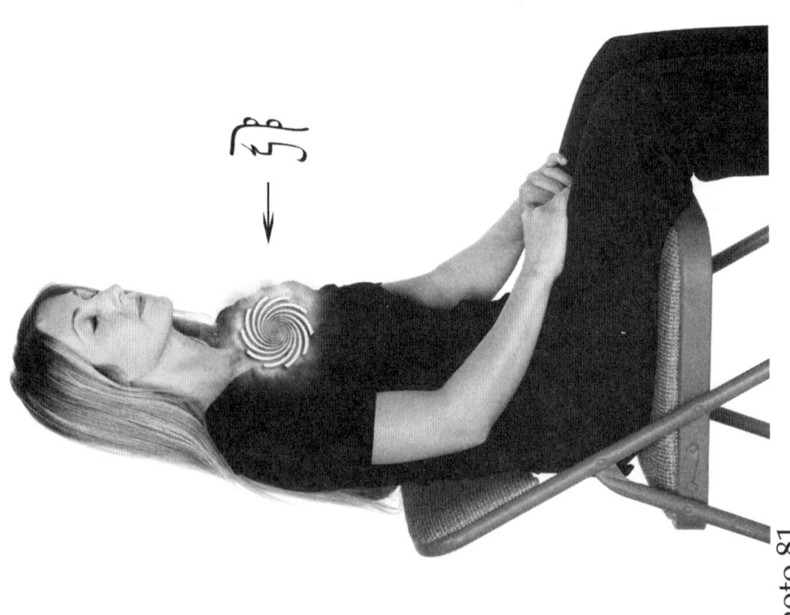

Photo 81

Photo 82

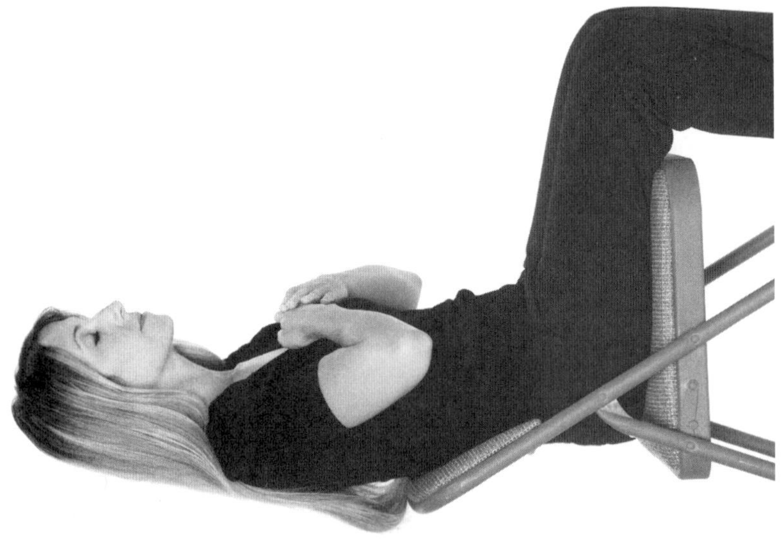

Photo 83

You can leave out the steps where you fill the Chakra with white or golden light and embed the Reiki Symbol of the person with whom you have shared the negative cord. But, I feel if you take the time to do this, there is less risk of cord re-attachment and you are helping the person to heal and move on.

Guiding a Disconnect Session

A Healer can help guide (facilitate) a relative, friend or client through a negative Psychic Cord disconnect session, and some people prefer the guidance. The steps are the same, but the Healer interacts with the person during the session by verbally leading them through the session step-by-step. The person who is having the session must dissolve the negative cord personally, but the Healer can fill the void with white or golden light, embed the Reiki Symbol and channel Reiki into the Chakra. The following are guidelines for guiding another person through a session.

Directions for Guiding a Session

You and the person for whom the session is being performed should begin by asking your Source, Higher Power, Universal Mind, Spirit Guide, Guardian Angel, etc., to help reveal any negative Psychic Cord attachments during the disconnect session.

Verbally guide the person through each step of the session. Here are a few examples of the wording you might use (or feel free to use your own wording as long as it is in context with the steps):

- "Please visualize the individual in front of you that you suspect you have a negative Psychic Cord with, and let me know when you have done so. Okay, now that you see the person, do you see a cord extending from this person attaching to one of your Chakras? If so, tell me which Chakra (Photo 84, Heart Chakra is used as an example) it is attached to and the color of the cord."

- "Now with strong, focused, conscious intent, visualize, know or imagine the negative cord connection to your Chakra being dissolved (Photo 85) with white or golden light. Please let me know when that is done."

- "Now do the same (Photo 86) for the person you have visualized. Do not worry about the remainder of the cord. Once it is disconnected from both of you, it will instantly dissolve by itself."

In Steps #8 and #9 you, as the facilitator, have an option of filling the person's void with the white or golden light, embedding the Reiki Symbol (Photo 87) and channeling Reiki (Photo 88) into their Chakra. If you decide you want to do this, have the person you are guiding do the last part of Step #8[13] first. After that is completed, you perform the first part of Step #8[14] and then finish up with Step #9.

Do not guide the person to the next step until he or she has stated or motioned that the step is completed and you have all the information (i.e., the color of the Chakra, to which Chakra the negative cord is attached, etc.) that is needed from that step.

---

[13] See Photo 82 for reference

[14] See Photo 81 for reference.

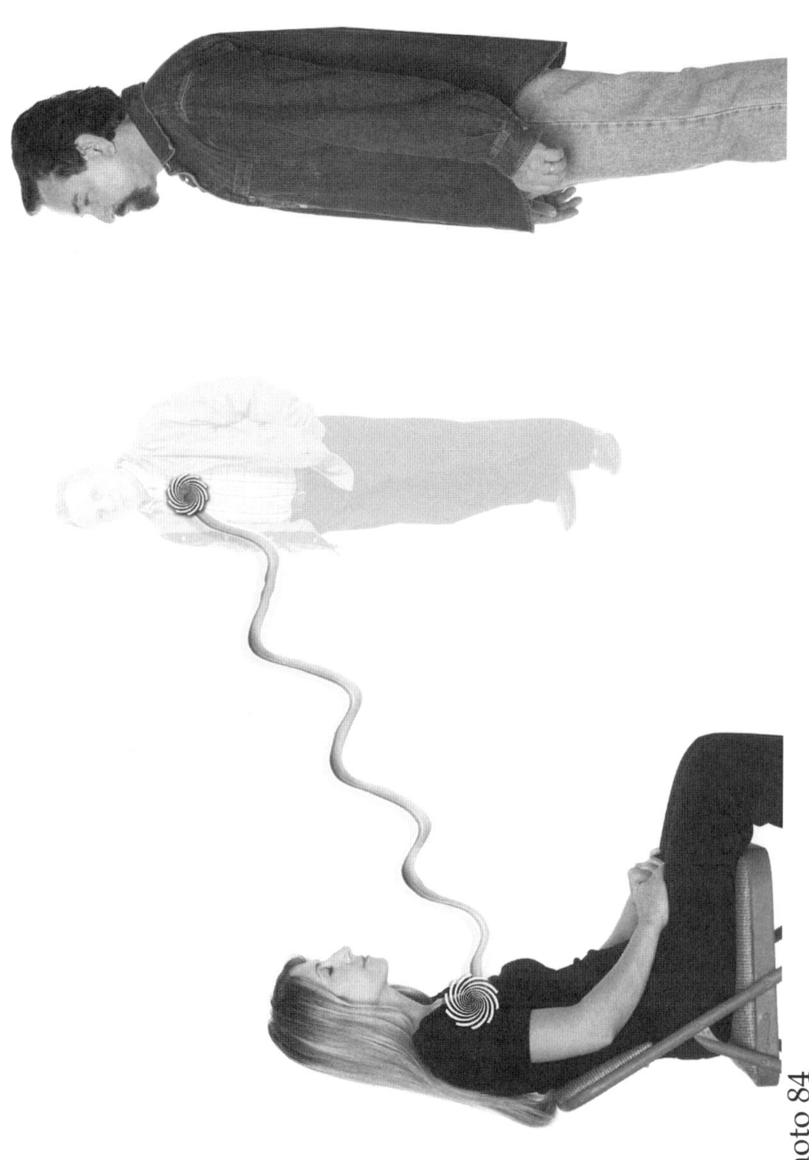

Photo 84

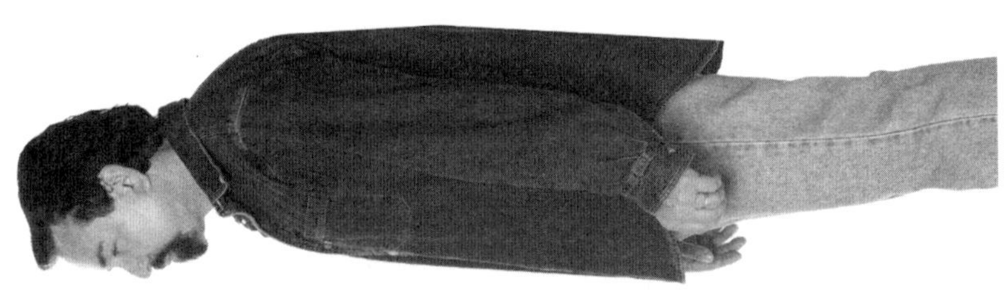

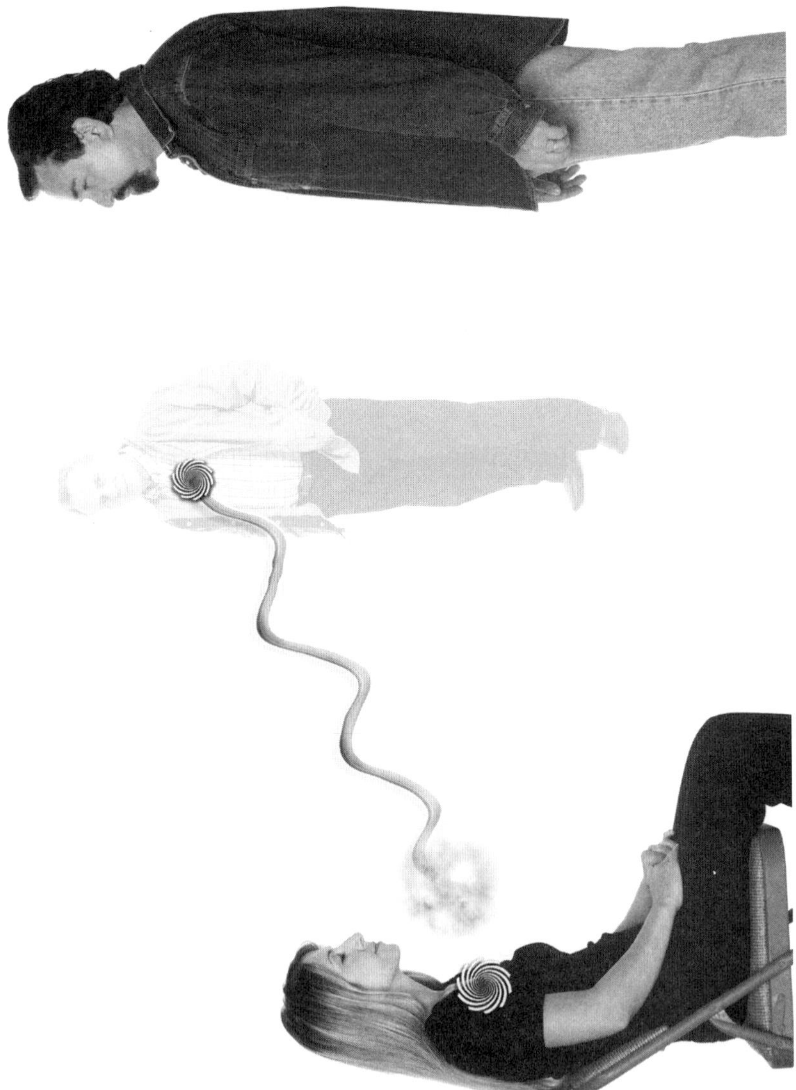

Photo 85

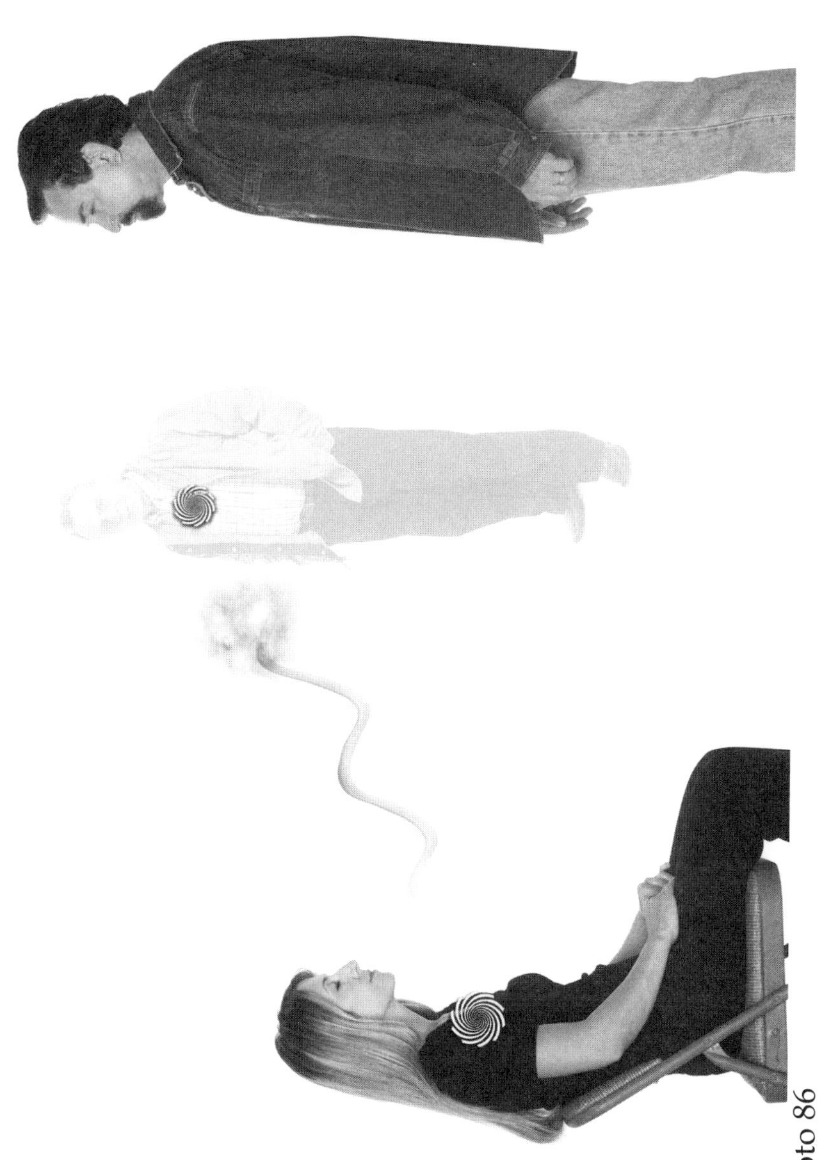

Photo 86

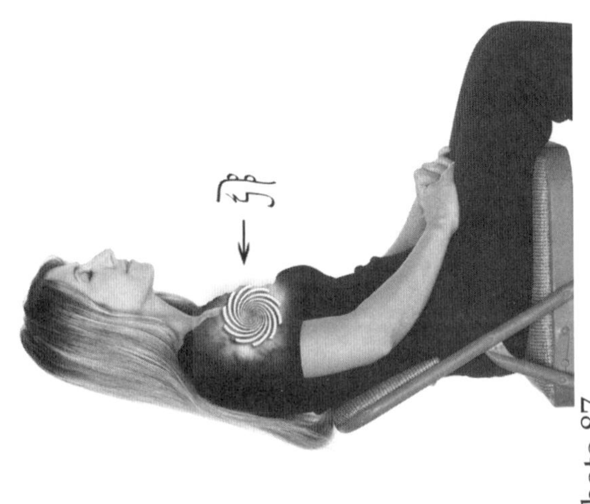

Photo 87

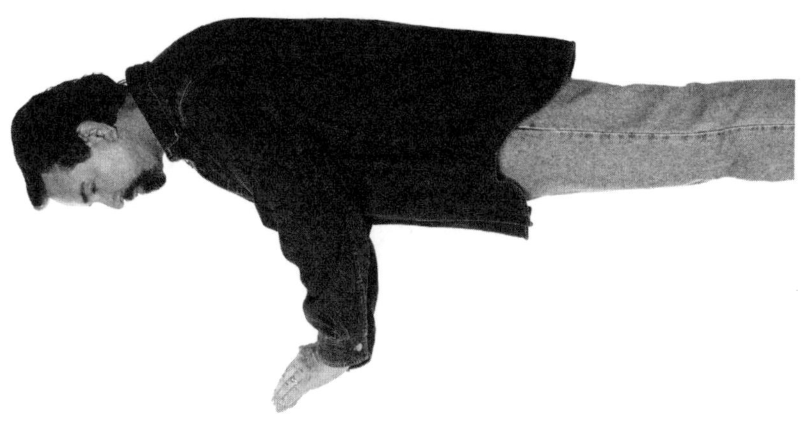

Photo 88

Knowledge has three degrees—opinion, science, illumination. The means or instrument of the first is sense; of the second, dialectic; of the third, intuition.

- Plotinus

Spirit Guides

You have to leave the city of your comfort
and go into the wilderness of your intuition.
What you'll discover will be wonderful.
What you'll discover is yourself.

- Alan Alda

Reiki Spirit Board

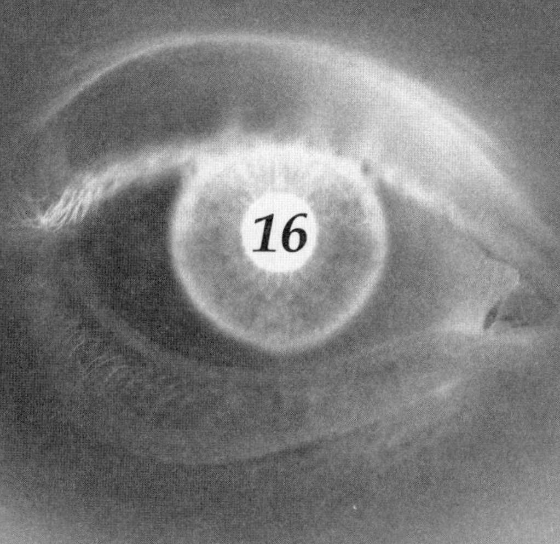

Your Spirit Guide

Many Reiki healers are already in contact with their Spirit Guides[15] and communicate with them in different ways. The reason Healers like to contact their Spirit Guides is to be able to ask for guidance in making decisions with healing and healing options for themselves and others.

[15] Non-physical souls who help us complete our life tasks and provide the spiritual assistance we need.

If you have a hard time contacting and receiving information from your Spirit Guide, a Reiki Spirit Board is a great spiritual aid in helping change that.

Reiki Spirit Board

A Reiki Spirit Board (Photo 89) is similar to most spirit boards. It is wooden and has 26 letters of the alphabet, the numbers 0-9, and the words "yes," "no," and "goodbye" engraved on it. The big difference between a spirit board and a Reiki Spirit Board is the Reiki Symbols are engraved on the Reiki Spirit Board.

When using the Reiki Spirit Board, the way the Spirit Guide communicates with you is straightforward - through the board and a pointer (I have the Power Symbol engraved on my pointer), also called a "planchette. " A pointer is a movable indicator that rests on the board and you lightly place your fingertips upon it. Once the fingertips are placed upon the pointer, a question is asked of the Spirit Guide. After a period of time the pointer will move about the board stopping at letters, numbers and symbols to convey the answer.

There are several beliefs on how this works. One, the pointer is actually moved by the direct force of the Spirit Guide. Two, the contacted Spirit Guide actually utilizes the eyes of the person using the pointer in order to point to the letters and words needed to form a message or answer.

Reiki
Spirit Board
Yes
No
A B C D E F G H I J K L M N
O P Q R S T U V W X Y Z
1 2 3 4 5 6 7 8
Good Bye

Photo 89

What I consider to be an asset in using a Reiki Spirit Board is you can ask your Spirit Guide questions, but you can respond like an ongoing conversation once you receive an answer. In other words, it is a back and forth flow of questions and answers with the possibility of the questions evolving as the contact progresses.

You will learn to use a Reiki Spirit Board by yourself[16] to connect with your Spirit Guide because of the personal nature of the contact. Do not be discouraged if contact does not happen the first few times. Keep trying. You will receive contact with your Spirit Guide eventually.

Make Your Own Reiki Spirit Board

It is relatively easy to make your own Reiki Spirit Board, and the directions follow. If you decide you do not want to make your own board, you can visit my website for information on how to purchase one.

- Decide on the size of your board and acquire a piece of wood of appropriate size. A typical board is at least 18″ x 10.″ You will need to include numbers 0-9, the alphabet, the words "yes," "no," and "goodbye," as well as the Reiki Symbols.

- Design the placement of your letters, numbers, words, and Reiki Symbols with a pencil via stencil or freehand. Make sure all letters, numbers and Reiki Symbols are

[16] A Reiki Spirit Board can also be used by two people to contact spirits. I explain how in my DVD "How to Contact Spirits Vol. 2." Spirits are people who have died and crossed over to the other side.

well-spaced so there will be no confusion as to where the pointer stops. Then paint, color or burn the design onto the board.

- The board needs to have a smooth, slick surface for the pointer to move easily. Coat the board with a few layers of polyurethane or cover it with glass.

- Pointers can be purchased from many sources on the Web, including e-Bay, or you can improvise a pointer by using a small, clear drinking glass.

The most common human error of today's world is not trusting your intuition.

- Edyta Sokolowska

Spirit Guide Contact

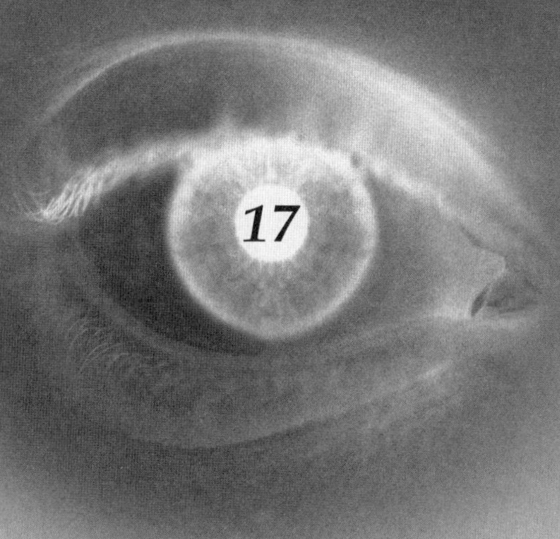

Know Your Spirit Guide

You should always know your Spirit Guide before using a Reiki Spirit Board. If you have not discovered your Spirit Guide yet, there are many simple methods[17] to do so. However, make sure you have received all three of the Reiki Psychic Attunements to help with the method you select.

[17] Several methods are given on pages 213 and 214.

Guidelines

The following are guidelines for using a Reiki Spirit Board when contacting your Spirit Guide.

- Use the board in a quiet area where you will not be disturbed. You can play meditation music at a low volume in the background, or just leave it silent.
- Be sure your board is clean and free of dust before using it.
- Clear the room[18] before and after contacting your Spirit Guide.
- Have lit candles and fresh flowers in the room.
- Make a list of questions you would like to ask your Spirit Guide before you start using the board. Keep the list next to you so you can read from it.
- You can place the board on a table, the floor or upon your knees, whatever way is the most comfortable for you.
- The contact should not last longer than sixty minutes. Save unanswered questions for the next contact.
- When using the pointer, place two, three, or four fingertips on each side of it. Once the contact starts, keep all fingertips on the pointer.

---

[18] Use the same method of clearing a room as in Chapter 4, page 37.

- Do not force the movement of the pointer. If it isn't responding to a light touch, your Spirit Guide isn't present yet.

- The pointer can move across the board slowly or quickly. If it moves quickly remain calm, and keep all fingertips on the pointer.

- Always use the Spirit Guide's name when asking a question.

- When receiving an answer to a question, each letter or number must be clearly pointed out.

- If the pointer is between letters or numbers, ask the Spirit Guide to reconfirm the letter or number and it should move to the correct one.

- When using the pointer, you're going to get the feeling it wants to stop at certain letters or numbers. Usually this is a subtle, intuitive impulse and you should go with it.

- You can use a recording device if you wish to revisit and interpret the answers at any time after the contact. This is especially helpful if the pointer is moving fast. Turn it on before you start, then call out the letters, numbers and symbols as the pointer stops.

Meditation helps you to grow your own intuitive faculty. It becomes very clear what is going to fulfill you, what is going to help you flower.

- Osho

Contact Your Spirit Guide

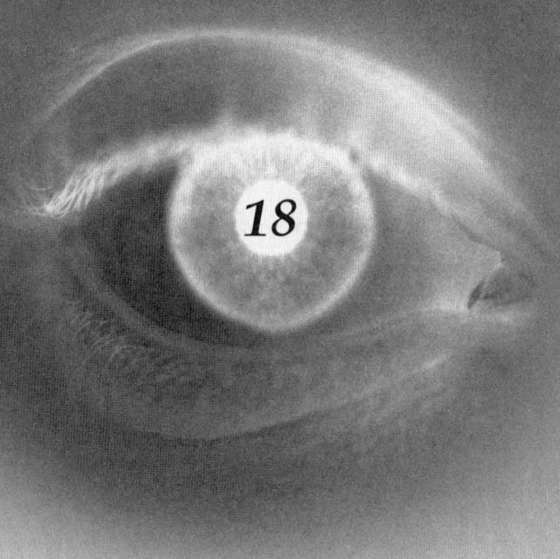

You Are Ready

You have completed all the guidelines from the previous chapter. The room is all set, you know your Spirit Guide and you have a list of questions prepared. You are now ready to make contact with your Spirit Guide.

Contact Your Spirit Guide Step-By-Step

1. The list of questions to be asked is placed next to you. Questions can be changed or added depending on the answers from your Spirit Guide.

2. If you are using a tape recorder, turn it on now.

3. Close your eyes and ask for guidance from whomever or whatever you believe (i.e., God, Higher Power, The Universe, Source, etc.) while you are using the Reiki Spirit Board.

4. After asking for guidance, take a few deep breaths and meditate a few moments, then open your eyes. Next, in a calm voice, call your Spirit Guide by name and ask it to come forward and make contact through the Reiki Spirit Board.

5. After asking your Spirit Guide to come forward, place fingertips from both of your hands on the pointer.

6. After your fingertips are placed on the pointer, ask the first question, either out loud or silently in your mind.

7. After one to five minutes, the pointer will commence to move and answer your question.

8. Once an answer is given, you can ask for more information or clarification, or ask a new question.

9. If the pointer is not moving after five minutes, start making a few slow circles on the board with the pointer, then stop. If there still is no response after a minute, ask the next question. Whenever there is no response to a question, use this format. Since it is between you and your Spirit Guide, I really don't know why there will be a response on some questions and none on others. I can only assume your Spirit Guide has a good reason for not giving you answers regarding certain questions. You can always ask the questions that aren't answered in a future contact, and maybe your Spirit Guide will feel you are ready for the answers at that time.

10. After fifty minutes, if you are still making contact it is time to close the contact. Ask your last question. Any unanswered questions can be asked in a future contact.

11. To close the contact at any time, thank your Spirit Guide for coming forward. The Spirit Guide should move the pointer to "goodbye" on the board in a few seconds. If this does not happen, then you move the pointer to "goodbye."

12. After thanking your Spirit Guide for coming forward and saying goodbye, the contact is over. Put out any candles and turn on the lights. If you recorded the contact, it can be played at your convenience to review your questions and the Spirit Guide's answers.

You can not truly comprehend the world you live in without feeling it.

- Edyta Sokolowska

Additional Information

**"The power of intuitive understanding
will protect you from harm
until the end of your days."**

- Lao Tzu

Reiki Symbols

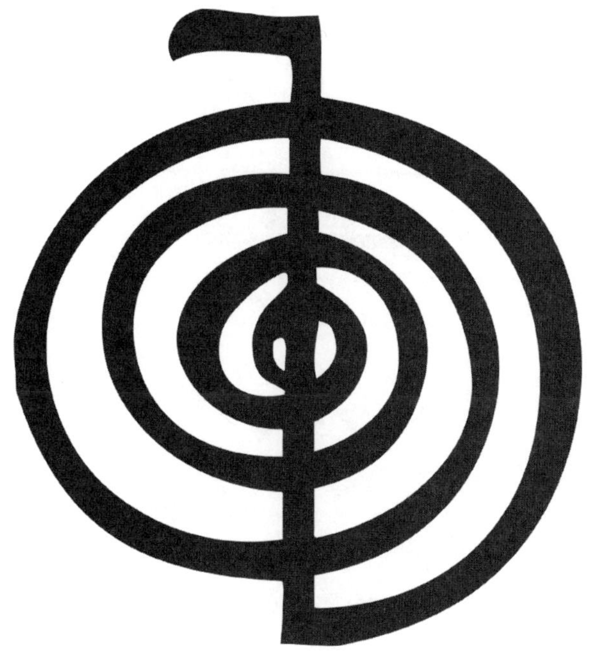

Cho Ku Rei

The Usui Power Symbol. It is also called the "Power Increase" Symbol. Its name is *Cho Ku Rei,* which means, *Put all the power in the universe here.* The Power Symbol has many uses when activated, but it is primarily used to increase the power of Reiki or to focus Reiki on a specific location, and also for protection.

Reiki Symbols

Hon Sha Ze Sho Nen

The Usui Long Distance Symbol. It is also referred to as the "Long Distance" and the "Absentee" Symbol. Its name is *Hon Sha Ze Sho Nen*. When activated with specific intent, Reiki can be sent anywhere, anytime in the past, present, or future. Distance, time, and space are not a barrier when you use this symbol.

Reiki Symbols

Sei He Ki

The Usui Mental/Emotional Symbol. It is also called the "Mental" or "Mental/Emotional/Addiction" Symbol. Its name is *Sei He Ki* and it means, *God and humanity become one.* This symbol has many uses when activated, but is commonly used in emotional, mental, and addictive healing situations.

Reiki Symbols

Dai Koo Myo

The Usui Reiki Master Symbol. Its name is *Dai Koo Myo*. The Master Symbol is the ultimate Reiki Symbol in all aspects. It intensifies Reiki, takes it to a higher level. When you activate other Reiki Symbols with the Master Symbol, the symbols are then taken to their highest level of effectiveness.

Psychic Debris

Excerpt from Reiki The Ultimate Guide Vol. 4
Past Lives & Soul Retrieval

Psychic Debris is referred to by many different names, which include "negative thought forms" and "emotional or mental blocks." Whatever it is called, most Healers are aware of it and agree that this phenomenon exists.

Psychic Debris can manifest as phobias, anger, fears, grief, anxiety or stress and can negatively affect your life. Psychic Debris eventually accumulates in some or all of your bodies - physical, mental, emotional and spiritual, thus creating blockages of your life force. The first place Psychic Debris usually manifests is in the mental, emotional and spiritual body in the Aura. If it is not released from this body and subsequently destroyed, it will eventually resonate down to and affect your physical body. This can cause a weakening of your immune system, resulting in illness and disease.

One of the sources that create Psychic Debris is unprocessed emotions. Emotions will accumulate over a period of time if they are not processed or released in a timely manner by the individual during the event(s) or circumstance(s). Normally these emotions (fear, grief, anger, hate, etc.) are necessary for the events and circumstances at the time they are generated. Processed and released in a timely manner, emotions are not negative and just a necessary part of the human experience for survival and healing. When emotions are held onto by the conscious or unconscious mind and not processed and released, they can accumulate in and around a person's body (Aura and Chakras) and manifest into Psychic Debris. This is when wellness challenges commence.

Another way Psychic Debris is created is by reliving unresolved life experience(s) repeatedly, remembering instances with great detail and emotion. These experiences have a negative emotional charge[19] linked to them. The charge can be anger, fear, anxiety, etc., so when a person relives the unresolved experience in their mind it sets off this negative emotional charge, which creates Psychic Debris. Unresolved life experience relived in the mind can be anything a person perceives as such. A few examples might be: not speaking up for yourself at work, not saying your peace to a loved one before death, a divorce with loose ends, an argument that's left open-ended and not showing up for a funeral.

Ultimately, Psychic Debris can be different for many individuals. It can be caused by many sources and circumstances unique to the person's life experience, current and past.

---

[19] An emotional charge is a strong emotional reaction to a circumstance, person, place or thing.

Your Spirit Guide

There are many ways to discover your Spirit Guide. There are guided imagery CDs, hundreds of visualization scripts and even books[20] devoted to the subject that can be found on the Internet, in book stores or libraries.

I will give two simple ways that usually help a person to discover their Spirit Guide. With both methods you might not receive your Spirit Guide's information while actually doing them, but they will set in motion the awareness and the intent that is needed for you to eventually receive the information. So, when you least expect it, your Spirit Guide information could float up to your conscious mind any time, during the day or night.

Try one method for a few weeks and if you have not received any results, try the other one. After trying both methods if you are not successful, just search the Internet, libraries or book stores for additional options.

1. Meditate. Start a meditation session by asking your Spirit Guide to reveal itself and their name to you during the meditation. Then meditate on discovering your Spirit Guide for about ten minutes. If your Spirit Guide is not revealed while you are meditating, keep doing it daily for a few weeks or until you have received the information.

2. Dream. Right before you go to sleep, mentally (silently) or out loud say, "Tonight I want to have a dream that will reveal my Spirit Guide and I will remember my dream

[20] I list a few in the bibliography page 217

when I awaken." Then, go to sleep. You will awaken either during the night or in the morning with what you asked for. If your Spirit Guide is not revealed in a dream, keep doing this method every night for a few weeks until you have the information.

Index

Bibliography

Anodea, Judith. Wheels of Life: A User's Guide to the Chakra System. Llewellyn Publications, 1999. ISBN-13: 978-0875423203.

Choquette, Sonia. Ask Your Guides: Connecting to Your Divine Support System. Hay House, 2007. ISBN-13: 978-1401907877.

Davies, Brenda. The 7 Healing Chakras Workbook. Ulysses Press, 2003. ISBN-13: 978-1569753675.

Eason, Cassandra. Contact Your Spirit Guides To Enrich Your Spirit Life. Quantum, 2005. ISBN-13: 978-0572031282.

Friedlander, John and Hemsher, Gloria. Basic Psychic Development: A User's Guide to Auras, Chakras & Clairvoyance. Weiser Books, 1999. ISBN-13: 978-1578630233.

Hewitt, William W. Psychic Development for Beginners: An Easy Guide to Releasing and Developing Your Psychic Abilities. Llewellyn Publications, 1996. ISBN-13: 978-1567183603.

Owens, Elizabeth. Spiritualism & Clairvoyance for Beginners: Simple Techniques to Develop Your Psychic Abilities. Llewellyn Publications, 2005. ISBN-13: 978-0738707075.

Pond, David. Chakras for Beginners: Honor Your Energy. Llewellyn Publications, 1999. ISBN-13: 978-1567185379.

Redmond, Layne .Chakra Meditation: Transformation through the Seven Energy Centers of the Body. Sounds True, 2004. ISBN-13: 978-1591791782.

Sanders, Pete A. You Are Psychic! The Free Soul Method. Fireside, 1999. ISBN-13: 978-0684857046

Webster, Richard. Spirit Guides & Angel Guardians: Contact Your Invisible Helpers. Llewellyn Publications, 2002. ISBN-13: 978-1567187953.

HOW TO ORDER DVDS, CDS, & BOOKS

To buy any of the following Books, DVDs or CDs check with your local bookstore, or www.healingreiki.com or email bodymindheal@aol.com, or call 949-263-4676.

BOOKS BY STEVE MURRAY

Cancer Guided Imagery Program
For Radiation, Chemotherapy, Surgery And Recovery

Reiki The Ultimate Guide
Learn Sacred Symbols and Attunements
Plus Reiki Secrets You Should Know

Successfully Preparing for Cancer Chemotherapy
Guided Imagery and Subliminal Program

Reiki The Ultimate Guide Vol. 4
Past Lives and Soul Retrieval
Remove Psychic Debris and Heal your life

Stop Eating Junk!
5 Minutes A Day-21 Day Program

Reiki The Ultimate Guide Vol. II
Learn Reiki Healing with Chakras
plus New Reiki Attunements for All Levels

Cancer Fear and Stress Relief Program

Reiki The Ultimate Guide Vol. 5
Learn New Psychic Attunements to Expand Psychic Abilities & Healing

DVDS BY STEVE MURRAY

Reiki Master Attunement
Become A Reiki Master

Reiki 2nd Level Attunement
Learn and Use the Reiki Sacred Symbols

A Reiki 1st
Aura and Chakra Attunement Performed

Successfully Preparing for Cancer Radiation
Guided Imagery and Subliminal Program

Reiki 1st Level Attunement
Give Healing Energy To Yourself and Others

Reiki Psychic Attunement
Open and Expand Your Psychic Abilities

Reiki Healing Attunement
Heal Emotional-Mental Physical-Spiritual Issues

Reiki Psychic Attunement Vol. 2
New Attunements to Expand Psychic Abilities

Preparing Mentally & Emotionally For Cancer Surgery
A Guided Imagery Program

Preparing Mentally & Emotionally For Cancer Surgery
A Guided Imagery Program

Preparing Mentally & Emotionally For Cancer Radiation
A Guided Imagery Program

Destroying Cancer Cells
Guided Imagery and Subliminal Program

Fear & Stress Relief Subliminal Program Let Your Unconscious Mind Do The Work!

Cancer Fear and Stress Relief Program

30-Day Subliminal Stop Smoking Program Let Your Unconscious Mind Do The Work!

Preparing Mentally & Emotionally For Cancer Chemotherapy
A Guided Imagery Program

Preparing Mentally & Emotionally For Cancer Recovery
A Guided Imagery Program

Pain Relief Subliminal Program
Let Your Unconscious Mind Do It!

30-Day Subliminal Weight Loss Program Let Your Unconscious Mind Do The Work!

Successfully Preparing for Cancer Chemotherapy
Guided Imagery and Subliminal Program

MUSIC CDs BY STEVE MURRAY

Reiki Healing Music Attunement Volume I

Reiki Psychic Music Attunement Volume I

Reiki Aura Music Attunement

Reiki Healing Music Attunement Volume II

Reiki Psychic Music Attunement Volume II

Reiki Chakra Music Attunement

DVDS BY BODY & MIND PRODUCTION

Learning To Read The Tarot Intuitively

Learning To Read The Symbolism Of The Tarot

How to Contact Spirits, Angels & Departed Loved Ones:
A step-by-step Guide

How to Contact Spirits Vol. 2
Learn to use a Spirit/Ouija Board and Hold a Séance

Mind Fitness Workout:
"Program the Mind for Weight Loss as you Exercise" Dance Workout

Mind Fitness Workout:
"Program the Mind for Weight Loss as you Exercise" Walking Workout

Mind Fitness Workout:
"Program the Mind for Weight Loss as you Exercise" Fitness Workout

More of what people are saying…

Again, I sincerely thank you for what you have written. Before I came across your first volume, I read other Reiki books, including books by Dr. Mikao Usui and others. While I'm grateful to have read things by the original creator, your books are head and shoulders above the rest. ***J.M.***

I found this book to be one of the best that I have read thus far on the subject of Reiki. The author leaves no stone unturned and reveals every aspect that could be revealed in written text. This book was well worth the money. ***S.B.***

Prolific writer and Reiki Master Steve Murray has once again given us a way to understand and heal ourselves of emotional baggage and psychic debris. I have read this manuscript three times to date and have experienced a sense of peace and understanding of who I am and where I come from. This practical self-help book will take you through the steps for understanding your past, present and future. ***H.P.***

Excellent for anyone who wants to learn Reiki. Steve's book is well written and instructions for attunements are very precise. I have all 4 of his books on Reiki and the 5th one pre-ordered. I too, am an Usui Reiki Master and intend on using his books in my classes. Bravo, Steve. ***K.Y.***

Once again, Steve Murray has written a wonderful book. It is clear and concise in its instructions for the past life and soul retrieval [sessions]. Both techniques are wonderful to use for your own healing and for others. ***M.H.***

Whether your goal is to work professionally with Reiki or to use it to heal and enhance your everyday life, you can't go wrong with Steve Murray's Books and DVDs. They are truly worth the investment! God bless Steve Murray! ***R.S.***

I would like to thank Steve Murray for providing these Reiki attunement programs. I have received 1st and 2nd degrees from his products and also from a live class. The experiences were very different but both were wonderful. I have not been able to raise the $1,000 required for my Masters Attunement. But Steve has made it very affordable to receive it. ***M.A.***

I have read all the books by Master Steve Murray, as well as taken his attunements, and I can assure you that there is nothing like this material in the market (and I have a huge Reiki Library). The books contain clear and concise information about all aspects of Reiki (most of which has been kept secret for no good reason at all - until now). The DVDs are as powerful as attunements in person. [This] material should be available to every Reiki Person in the world. ***T.W.***

I really liked the book - it was an easy read. The chapters were short and informative which kept me focused. It answered the questions I had about Reiki in a how-to manner. It gives you in depth directions and illustrations on how to do Attunements. Steve Murray's knowledge and insight is really reflected in the book's words. Anyone interested in learning Reiki should get this book. ***D.D.***

Steve Murray is a great educator and healer in the field of Reiki. He has brought the blessings of Reiki to all in a clear, consistent, beautifully organized, and easy to understand format. The books are a great asset to refer to as you begin to practice and implement Reiki healings. Steve Murray has given a blessing to humanity by unfolding the magnificent flower of Reiki to all of humanity. Love and Gratitude. ***L.D.***

If you're a seeker of knowledge, this book is for you. Whether it is Reiki, or past lives, you will learn great techniques in this book. We highly recommend Steve's books and DVDs. ***E.S.***

About the Author

Steve Murray is an experienced Usui Reiki Master and the author of the best selling Reiki The Ultimate Guide series. He also has a series of 25 self-healing programs on DVD. The DVD subjects include Reiki Attunements; Cancer Guided Imagery; weight loss, pain, fear, and stress relief, just to name a few. He has produced six Reiki CDs for healing, and for Aura, Chakras and psychic sessions.

“Shanti” Steve Murray